I0116509

How to Talk Politics without Arguing
"I Think I'm Right, but I Could Be Wrong"

By Constantinos E. Scaros, JD, PhD
Bonus Segment by Amanda Keating, PsyD

To the good Americans; that's almost all of them

Copyright © 2021 by Constantinos E. Scaros

Cover design by Camille Rossi Petruccio, Impress Graphic Design

All rights reserved. Duplication of any part of this book or cover requires permission of the author.

ISBN: 9780578919676

Atalanta Publishing
Bespoke Book Crafting

Atalantapublishing.com

Table of Contents

Constantinos E. ("Dino") Scaros is the author of several books covering many contemporary issues. Visit his website, www.listentodino.com for a complete list of his books.

Praise for Dino Scaros and His Books

"The watchdog of the American media"
Congressman Gus Bilirakis (from the Foreword to *Trumped-Up Charges!*)

"Required reading for all Republicans"
Michael Dukakis (from *Grumpy Old Party*)

"Multiple perspectives rooted in common sense"
John Catsimatidis, Jr., Principal of Red Apple Group (from the Foreword to *Grumpy Old Party*)

"Instead of spending all that money on political advisors, every Republican should read this book instead!"
Tricia Erickson, author of *Can Mitt Romney Serve Two Masters?* (from *Grumpy Old Party*)

"Great no matter which side you come from" (Amazon 5-star review of *Trumped-Up Charges!*)

"You don't have to be a Trump supporter to read this book" (Amazon 5-star review of *Trumped-Up Charges!*)

"Easily the most honest book about the issue of illegal immigration" (Amazon 5-star review of *Stop Calling Them "Immigrants"*)

"Every American should read this book" (Amazon 5-star review of *Stop Calling Them "Immigrants"*)

"I love this book. Thank you" (Amazon 5-star review of *Learning about Immigration Law*)

PREFACE

Who am I, and Why Should You Consider Taking Advice from Me?

This is a "how-to" book. How-to books are very popular, and for good reason. People want advice. They want to figure out how to solve a problem, accomplish a goal, overcome a dilemma, experience more joy, better health, make more money, succeed in a personal relationship, and a host of other reasons. The question that comes to mind when I encounter such a book is: "who is this author and why should I consider taking advice from him/her?" I think that's a good question, and one you should be asking as well. So, if you take a couple of minutes and allow me to tell you a little bit about myself, I hope you'll want to read on.

I am a presidential historian with a bachelor's degree in political science and a master's and PhD in history. I've been studying presidents ever since I was a kid. As an adult I've held many different types of jobs, but three of my fields in particular demand objectivity and evenhandedness, even though, unfortunately, a lot of people in each of them don't quite understand that. They are: journalism, education, and history. Like most people, I have opinions—strongly held ones at times—about food, music, sports, and many other things, including politics. But when I write a news article, when I teach a class, or when I am chronicling a historical account, I leave those opinions on the doorstep, where they belong. Readers of news about the present or past, and students in a school setting should not have their minds made up for them. Journalists, educators, and historians are obligated to inform but must resist the temptation to persuade.

Next, I am not a political extremist. In my life I have voted for Democrats, Republicans, independents, and third party candidates. I have plenty of praise, and criticism, to give any president, to varying degrees, of course. And I am also the first to rush to the defense of any president who I think is being judged unfairly, and because of his position is an easy target to scapegoat. I am not prone to blind, unconditional partisanship, nor do I defend the "home team" at any cost. Perhaps most importantly of all, I have a definite preference for one of these two very different sayings: the first is: "winning isn't everything, it's the only thing" and the second is "it's not whether you win or lose, it's how you play the game." To me, the second is much more meaningful. Don't get me wrong, I like winning just as much as the next person, but I'm not going to stubbornly dismiss logic staring me in the face just to win an argument. In fact, a motto by which I live, and is the title of Chapter 1, is "I think I'm right, but I could be wrong." And I'm surely not going to lie, cheat, or steal in order to win, and that includes not knowingly or recklessly passing along false information that helps my argument. Along those lines, if ever I write something about which I'm wrong, I would hope someone would point it out to me because another adage I follow is: "I reserve the right to be smarter tomorrow than I am today."

Finally, I am very careful to be as accurate as possible with all factual information that I present, and also to communicate it in a crystal-clear manner so that there is no doubt about what message I intend to convey. It all builds up to the final chapter, which is about how to have a political conversation without arguing.

I hope this preface gives you enough encouragement to continue reading. On we go!

INTRODUCTION

Our Long, Political Nightmare

On August 9, 1974, Richard Nixon resigned from the presidency of the United States, the only instance when such a thing has happened. Shortly thereafter, Nixon's vice president, Gerald Ford, took the oath of office and became the 38th president of the United States. Ford then gave a speech in which he used these words to describe how Nixon's resignation marked an end to the tumultuous multiyear scandal that wrecked his presidency: "our long, national nightmare is over."

On January 20, 2021, Donald Trump's presidency came to an end, and that of his successor, Joe Biden, began. Tens of millions of Americans were overjoyed to see Trump go, and many surely would agree that "our long, political nightmare is over." Except, it isn't. It's far from over. I can't quite say it's only just begun, because, actually, it has been blazing for decades.

Biden's three predecessors, Presidents George W. Bush (43, the son), Barack Obama, and Trump, were all labeled "dividers" by a large number of their disparagers. Each had supporters who would insist that the president in question did his best to bring the country together, but his political opponents didn't give him a chance. Regardless of who's right and who's wrong, the fact remains that our country was bitterly divided *before* any of these three became president. The Bush-Gore race of 2000 is a clear indicator, as the election hinged upon a few hundred votes in

Florida, with that state's winner securing enough electoral votes to amass the necessary 270. Bush was declared the victor on Election Night by the major networks, prompting Gore to call him to concede, as per tradition. A short while later, Gore called back in quite an awkward moment, retracting his concession because he hadn't realized how incredibly tight the Florida race was. A mandatory recount followed, as did a later third count requested by Gore. All three counts (including the original) were for Bush, by tiny margins. Gore wanted an additional and more expansive recount, but the Bush team said enough is enough. Gore challenged the election in federal court, which ruled in Bush's favor. Gore won on appeal, and the matter went before the U.S. Supreme Court, which ordered the recounts to stop in order to certify the election by the statutory deadline. Approximately half the country rooting for Bush agreed. Their man had won three counts; how many more recounts, they complained, did Gore want? The other half of the country saw things much differently, sure that it was Gore who had prevailed, and more extensive recounts would prove it, but that the Supreme Court showed partisan favoritism (most of the justices had been appointed by Republican presidents) by ruling in favor of the Republican candidate. There was much bitterness in the country for months that followed, only to be simmered by the terrorist attacks of September 11, 2001, which strongly but briefly saw the nation converge in a rare instance of unity. Twenty years later, the country is just as divided politically, but the rancor is even worse. When Bush left office in January 2009 and Obama was inaugurated, the

Bush-bashers breathed a sigh of relief, blaming him for having pitted one party against the other, and confident that Obama would bring the very hope and change he promised. Eight years later, when Obama left and Trump took over, same thing, different group. Trump's followers were euphoric that finally, a non-politician who tells it like it is would "drain the swamp" in Washington, yet things remain as divided as ever. Considering, then, that the election of 2000 took place while Bill Clinton was still president, we have had four presidents since then—two Democrats, two Republicans—and no unity achieved by any of them.

Divided vs. Despiteful

As we proceed, it is important to know that although they often go hand-in-hand, there is a difference between politics that are divided vs. despiteful. People can be divided in their views but remain civil, respectful, and even friendly about it. The problem is that a divided America has also caused those on opposite political and ideological sides to become abrasive, belligerent, and downright cruel toward one another.

There have been ebbs and flows in American politics from the nation's early days, one of the most famous political feuds having been between the second and third presidents, respectively, John Adams and Thomas Jefferson. But in recent times, the vitriol didn't kick into high gear until the mid-1990s. Each political party will point the finger at the other, but both are to blame. Republicans treated Bill Clinton noticeably harshly. Democrats then did worse to George W. Bush, and

Republicans, in turn, even worse to Barack Obama. I remember predicting sometime around 2012 or 2013, in the middle of Obama's presidency, that we are in a cycle of high-octane political warfare, and the next president, after Obama, would be treated even worse. That next president turned out to be Donald Trump, and while many acknowledge how intensely he's been criticized, they add that he brought it on himself. That may be the case to some extent, but back when I had made that prediction about how disrespectfully the 45th president of the United States would be treated by the opposing party, hardly anyone even had any inkling that it would have been the controversial Trump.

The true test of whether the tide will turn this time will be how the Republicans treat Biden. Unlike Trump, Biden is not particularly combative. He does not relish in mixing it up with his political rivals. When they hit him with a verbal blow, he doesn't hit back twice as hard; like most politicians, Biden tends to shrug it off. Then again, so did Clinton, Bush, and Obama most of the time, and yet they didn't escape the venom hurled by the other side.

The 1980s is in our relatively recent past but in terms of discourse, it seems like a million years ago. That's when President Reagan and House Speaker Tip O'Neill, the former a transformational leader who ushered in conservatism and the latter one of Congress' preeminent liberal lions for decades, battled it out by day and then joined each other for a beer after work. That's when differences were ideological, not personal. That camaraderie was not limited to elected officials; it extended to the public as well. Siblings, cousins, friends, spouses, neighbors, and coworkers teased each other about their favorite candidates, much like sports fans of rival teams kid each other good-naturedly about who's going to win the game. Nowadays, "unfriending"—the practice of disconnecting on social media which, effectively, often means not being on any kind of speaking terms, at least for the time being—has permeated our vocabulary. Not since the Civil War has there been such deep division based on political affiliation.

Functioning Well in Bad Weather

Where this book differs from others on the topic is that others focus on how to unite the country politically. While that is a noble idea, it is neither realistic nor necessary. It is ok for people to have opposing views about how to move forward. The key, however, is to embrace folks with alternative points of view, not condemn them. Consider this analogy, to illustrate: I remember taking a trip to Canada several years ago. Friends there explained to me that blizzards that dump a few feet of snow on the ground are so common there, that plowing the big mess is second nature to Canadians. That is very different from the chaos that often breaks out in a good-sized city in the American South that's been surprised by a rare snowstorm. The answer to how to deal with bad weather shouldn't be to hope for good weather instead, it should be to learn how to function smoothly and efficiently even when the weather is bad.

Well-prepared cities don't fear snowstorms, they're ready for them. Similarly, we shouldn't look at differing points of view as problematic. Instead, we should embrace them as opportunities to advance intellectual growth through competing ideas, and learn how to discuss our differences peacefully, cordially, and amicably.

Before we move on, keep in mind that people who are happy, smiling, and friendly toward one another aren't necessarily good and kind. Maybe they really are, but it could just be that they agree with one another. The real challenge, then, is not to get everyone to agree with everyone else, but rather to teach them how to disagree kindly and respectfully.

Up next, Chapter 1 explores the phrase we introduced in the preface, "I think I'm right, but I could be wrong," a mindset that embodies this book's general message.

CHAPTER 1

"I Think I'm Right, but I Could Be Wrong"

The first step to talking politics without arguing is being able to say this about yourself in any— yes, *any*—situation: "I think I'm right, but I could be wrong."

A lot of people have three big problems with being wrong. One is that they hate being wrong, especially if they've been proven wrong—we'll get to that one later on. The second big problem is that they are often unable to realize when they're wrong, and third, which is the one we'll discuss right away, is that they can't even imagine the possibility that they could be wrong. That third problem in many ways is the most fascinating of all: people's inability to view the statistical probability that at some point they'll make some mistakes.

Granted, many folks lack self-confidence, but even then, they are confident in their judgment. For example, several years ago I used to help a friend of mine run a very popular Friday night karaoke show in New York City, during the height of karaoke's rise in popularity across America. The show was held inside a bar/restaurant, and almost every week there were some folks who went there to eat and drink but were curious enough to stick around to watch the show. I befriended many of them and would encourage them to sing, and very often their response was: "oh, no, I'm a terrible singer." They were convinced they'd sound horrible, but in most cases, they were wrong.

Many received thunderous cheers, much to their amazement. Once they finished singing, they couldn't wait for their turns to sing again. They were surprised—surprised to have been wrong.

Try this exercise right now: think about five times in your life when you were wrong about something. Really wrong. When you miscalculated, misjudged, and misunderstood a person, an event, or a situation. Specifically, think about instances when you had a discussion with someone else about how to fix a particular problem or speculate about some occurrence. Will the refrigerator fit through the front door? Is this restaurant going to be good? Should we go there on vacation? Seriously. <u>Don't just keep reading; it's important to think about five such instances, now.</u>

People tend to remember successes, but they either block failures out of their minds or keep the information to themselves. Someone who plays the stock market or otherwise gambles won't miss a chance to talk about good fortune. But rarely will you hear about that person's losses. People will brag about the business deals they closed due to their savvy, but not the ones they blew because of their own blunders. They'll tell you about the time they believed at the beginning of the season when no one else did, that a certain sports team would win the championship. But they won't often admit the times when they were way off base. That's because it's human nature for people not to want to be wrong, and to have enough of a problem with it that oftentimes they'll try to sweep their mistakes under the rug.

On February 7, 2021, the Tampa Bay Buccaneers (Bucs) defeated the Kansas City Chiefs to win professional football's championship, the Super Bowl (LV, *i.e.*, 55). Before the season started, I predicted the Bucs would win. They had just acquired legendary quarterback Tom Brady from the New England Patriots, and added major offensive and defensive weapons to help him lead them to a championship. I could stop right there with the story and look like a genius, but I'm not like that; I'll give you the second part too: I also predicted that the Bucs would play the Patriots in the Super Bowl who, after all, still had coaching great Bill Belichick and had just acquired an extremely athletic quarterback with a potentially great upside, Cam Newton. Boy was I wrong on that one! The Patriots had their first losing season in eons, and not only did they not qualify for the Super Bowl, but they didn't even make the playoffs! But far too many people aren't comfortable with admitting when they were wrong. They really ought to try doing so, it's not so bad.

A way to get used to feeling more comfortable with being wrong is to actually set yourself up to be wrong and to be happy about it. To say, ahead of time, "I hope I'm wrong." An easy way to do that is to choose an outcome about which you are pessimistic. For example, I remember becoming overwhelmed by an irrational fear as I was getting ready to graduate from law school. Generally, my law school experience was a happy one, particularly because of the lifelong friendships I made and the fun we all had together when we weren't in class or hitting the books. I looked forward to graduation, which would happen in a few days, but final grades weren't announced yet.

One of my friends said to me: "I'm not going to relax until I see my final grades," which got me to thinking: "what if I fail one of my final exams? What will I tell my family, who are coming to graduation, that I didn't graduate because I failed? And what about all of my classmates? We were all looking forward to celebrating together, and now I'll have to stay home?" It was an irrational fear because I had never failed a class, in law school or elsewhere, but the possibility of such a calamity stayed in my mind until I got the good news that I had passed all of my classes and I would march across that stage on Graduation Day. Boy, was I happy to be wrong!

To review, four words that epitomize true open-mindedness are: "I could be wrong." They can be prefaced with "I think I'm right," which justifies defending a particular point in the first place. Taken together, "I think I'm right, but I could be wrong" captures the spirit of intellectual honesty and integrity. If everyone involved in a discussion would begin by making that proclamation, acknowledging the very real possibility of being wrong, then there could be mutual respect among the whole group. Just as "I could be wrong" are four of the most wonderful words to declare, perhaps the seven worst words to utter are: "you're not going to change my mind." Nothing screams narrowmindedness more than a phrase that essentially forewarns the others that "my mind is made up because I know I'm right. So, either agree with me or don't bother speaking."

A closely related counterproductive phrase is: "I don't want to talk about it." However, there is a time and a place for that one. If it is utilized so as to diffuse a potentially volatile, abrasive situation, then silence may be the best option. But if someone simply shuts down about a particular issue and says "I don't want to talk about it," that basically slams the door on the opportunity to be heard and often implies the aforementioned "you're not going to change my mind" shout.

A good, productive, constructive conversation ought to be about being more informed once it has concluded, and the way to go about it is to leave emotions behind and not to go into it trying to win. Far too often, people don't just talk past one another, but in their absolutist conclusion that they must be right try to convince the other to join their way of thinking instead of working together to achieve a common goal. That could have undesirable consequences for both. Here's a simple example, to illustrate: suppose that you and your spouse are in the car, wanting to get from Point A to Point B, which is more or less a three-hour drive. You insist that Road 1 is the best way to get there, while your spouse is just as convinced that Road 2 is the ideal path to take. Logically, it would seem that your goal is a common one: to get to your destination in as little time as possible and to encounter the least amount of aggravation (such as traffic, potholes, dangerous neighborhoods, etc.). Instead, if you are so confident that your way is right, you might make arguments so passionate and rooted in emotion that you forego common sense. Your spouse may do the same. Instead, you decide to use GPS (Global Positioning System) to determine a few important pieces of information, such as, which road is a longer distance in terms of miles, and which is showing a faster arrival time. Road 1, your way, shows the trip is estimated to take two hours and 40 minutes. Your spouse's way, Road 2, shows two hours and 50 minutes. However, it saves 35 miles. You both know that Road 2 is a narrower road and there are some lights, whereas Road 1 is all highway. What you both encounter, though, is Road 3. It is the shortest distance of all, and shows a drive time of just two hours and 20 minutes! You both exclaim: "looks like we have a winner!" Rather than try to out-argue (or, shout-argue) the other, you had a discussion that led to a better way, and you both agreed. Now, what's wrong with doing that with politics?

Being comfortable with the "I could be wrong" concept, we'll keep that in our pocket as we turn to Chapter 2 to explore two people at the forefront of the storm of political arguments.

CHAPTER 2

Donald Trump and Nancy Pelosi

"Donald Trump, Nancy Pelosi." There, I said it. Let's throw those names out there and put our cards on the table. As of this writing, they are probably the two most polarizing names in politics today. Most people clearly prefer one over the other, even though many have negative feelings about both.

Before we proceed, keep in mind that "Trump" and "Pelosi" are mere examples of the moment. They can easily be interchanged with other politicians of the past (or of the future from this writing); it's just that right now, they happen to be the two highest-profile political lightning rods. For instance, when I was assigned to teach a political science course in the mid-1990s, I selected two books for students to read during the semester: *Reason to Believe* by Mario Cuomo, and *To Renew America* by Newt Gingrich. Cuomo had been governor of New York State for several years (his son Andrew is currently governor of that state), and remained a nationally recognized figure and a symbol of liberal Democratic ideology (political philosophy). Gingrich was Speaker of the U.S. House of Representatives at the time, and a prime example of post-Reagan populist conservatism. They were the political lightning rods of their time, but no longer are. For one thing, Cuomo passed away a few years ago, and Gingrich, now in his late seventies, hasn't held elected office in over 20 years.

So, for the purposes of this discussion, when we discuss "Trump" and "Pelosi" we are talking about those two actual individuals, although the concept can apply to anyone.

Donald Trump is the 45th president of the United States. He ran and won as a Republican in 2016, and he served from January 2017 to January 2021, losing his reelection bid in 2020 to Joe Biden. Nancy Pelosi, a Democrat representing the state of California, is Speaker of the U.S. House of Representatives. They are a good case study of how the same politician can be viewed very differently depending on the beholder. Trump supporters see him as perhaps America's last, best hope to combat an establishmentarian oligarchy comprised of both major political parties, the media, academia, Hollywood, and Wall Street. They celebrate that he is not a career politician, isn't in politics for the money, and brings an outside-the-box business entrepreneurial mindset to governing. His critics see him as incompetent, erratic, egotistical, and overwhelmed at best; racist, sexist, Islamophobic, fascistic, unhinged, and criminally culpable at worst.

Pelosi's fans celebrate her as a pioneer trailblazer, savvy political grandmaster, champion of justice and fairness, and guardian of the principles upon which this nation was founded, protecting them from the threat of a Trump-inspired assault on our democracy. Her critics envision her as alarmingly leftist, wicked, vengeful, petty, ditzy, incompetent, coddled, and vastly overrated.

On January 6, 2021, two weeks before the end of Trump's presidency, Trump spoke in front of tens of thousands who had gathered from all over the country at a rally in Washington, DC, walking distance from the U.S. Capitol building, based on the theme Save America, which was a protest of the 2020 presidential election result's legitimacy. Shortly after that speech, hundreds of those individuals illegally entered the Capitol, some violently overpowering police in the process, and several of them vandalized the offices of senators and representatives. Some died in the melee and others were injured. Many blamed Trump for inciting the attack because of his highly charged rhetoric, while others insisted that Trump wanted a massive, loud protest demonstration, but one that was legal and nonviolent. Pelosi took the former view and led the way for Trump's impeachment by the House, which was successfully accomplished and the second (a record) of his presidency. Critics railed that it was a frivolous partisan witch hunt because the next step in the process, a trial in the Senate, was pointless because it would not take place until after January 20, when Trump no longer would be president anyway. Supporters, conversely, argued not only that the impeachment was absolutely warranted, but that if convicted at the trial, the Senate could vote to bar Trump from ever holding public office again. The two sides clashed about whether such a possibility is political censorship or in the best interest of the nation as a whole. Ultimately, the Democrat-controlled Senate voted that it was constitutional to proceed with the impeachment trial, but Trump was acquitted on February 13, because only 57 senators voted to convict, and 67 (two-thirds) are needed. The vote was overwhelmingly partisan, as 100 percent of Democrats voted to impeach, and 86 percent of Republicans voted to acquit.

Consequently, many view Trump as a victimized martyr and Nancy Pelosi as a tyrant. They continue to believe the election was stolen, and even if it wasn't, the Democrats don't want to know the truth because their goal is to establish one-party domination and silence the Trump movement forever, aided by "Never Trumper" Republicans. Many on the opposite side view the Capitol invasion as the culmination of Trump's tolerance, if not encouragement, of angry, white supremacist deadly mobs bent on violently overthrowing the government, and Pelosi is the leader of the noble charge to rescue America from such heinous monsters.

Then, there is a large group in the middle. One that examines each aspect of this entire phenomenon carefully and draws conclusions issue by issue, rather than accepting the "Trump" or "Pelosi" side completely without exception. It is a group that can be critical of the side it normally supports, just as it can be complimentary toward the one it usually opposes, and we will discuss some of that later on, and particularly in the final chapter. It is such sensible people who I think will most appreciate this book, and if you're reading this now, you're probably part of that big group, and I hope that once you're done reading it, you'll pass it along to those in your circle of family, friends, and acquaintances currently occupying one of the rigid fringes.

CHAPTER 3

Why We Talk Politics in the First Place

There are many reasons why people talk to each other. We rarely stop and think ahead of time *why* we want to have a conversation. Instead, we simply open our mouths and start flapping our gums. Let's stop and think about it now: why do we have conversations? What is our goal? Let's take a look at some possibilities: first, there is common lamentation (sorrow). People will often share how awful they feel about a certain event. For instance, if dozens of people die in an earthquake somewhere far away, someone might say: "did you see what happened on the news?" "Horrible!" might exclaim another person. "It's such a shame," a third might add. In that scenario, everyone involved in the conversation is upset that people died in an earthquake; no one is happy about it. Conversely, the purpose could be to express common joy. "Sue just gave birth to a beautiful baby girl!" "That's great news!" "Oh, I can't wait to see the baby!" Everyone is delighted about Sue's new baby. In either situation, the reason people start talking is to express their emotions out loud, not to try to change someone's mind. The folks who started those two conversations certainly didn't think that anyone was going to disagree with their opinion, let alone start an argument about it. However, that's not the case when the discussion turns to politics.

Often times, people start political arguments unwittingly. Sticking with "Trump" and "Pelosi" as our opposing political lightning rods, imagine someone says: "all these people who voted for Trump are idiots," or "anyone who supports Pelosi must really hate America." The former statement spoken in front of Trump supporters or the latter to Pelosi fans could result in an argument, or at least an intensely abrasive reply. Having assumed that their statements would have been unanimously echoed—as if they were about sorrow for earthquake victims or joy for the birth of a baby—those making the original statements might then think to themselves: "I didn't expect this to turn into an argument." That assumption is usually a symptom of lacking the "I think I'm right, but I could be wrong" mindset. Those who are so stubbornly set in their ways think their way of thinking is pristinely flawless and so if they say their piece out loud, how can anyone possibly disagree? Part of talking politics without arguing, then, is to recognize that rare is the point that does not elicit a counterpoint.

Another reason—a very big one—why people enter into discussions, particularly political ones, is to persuade. Granted, some people talk politics simply for the art of the debate, or because they derive some sort of pleasure from being contrarian (not many of them are reading this book). But most who bring up politics realize that they're likely to encounter an opposing view but are so sure that they're right, and so they'll persuade the other person to see their way of thinking. Part of their attempted political proselytizing stems from a strong belief that their point of view is objectively more correct and more logical, and so their interlocutors (the others in the conversation) are bound to see the light once they are exposed to it.

The next section will help to explain why that's not likely to be the case.

Why We Prefer Certain Politicians

Americans, more or less, share the same good values. We'll talk about that later on. But shared values does not necessarily mean shared priorities. Take law enforcement, for instance: the overwhelming majority of Americans are against crime *and also* against police brutality. However, two people who share those values may rank them in different orders of importance. Suppose that the president is considering appointing a new attorney general. One of these two individuals might say: "I hope it's someone who will really fight crime hard. There's no excuse for people killing people. It's got to stop," whereas the other might emphasize: "I hope he or she will focus on ending police brutality. The police are too aggressive and they intimidate the people they are supposed to be serving, especially persons of color. We need to feel safe around our police, not fearful." Although both support safety and respect, one would likely prefer a "law-and-order" focused attorney general, and the other would rather have a "social justice" advocate. It doesn't mean that the former doesn't care about police brutality and that the latter is indifferent to crime. But that's when the arguing begins, when the two simply don't understand each other, and trade accusations: "Don't you understand how much crime there is? It's more important not to be murdered than not to be roughed up a little bit because of race." Or, "you care nothing about how persons of color, particularly African-Americans, have to look over their shoulder constantly in fear of the police. As long as the police protect you, you don't really care about anybody else."

Another reason we choose to vote for Candidate A instead of Candidate B is confidence in him or her. Politicians are typically going to promise us the moon; you'll be hard-pressed to find a candidate on the campaign trail who'll say: "Vote for me, but I'm not really going to change anything for you. In fact, your life may get even worse. It's not that I don't want to help you, it's just that most of the problems out there are really tough to solve. So many others have tried and failed, what makes you think I'll be any better? I mean, I'll give it a try, but I can't make any promises." While some may appreciate the refreshing honesty, most voters want to be inspired and reassured. Therefore, they'll probably never hear a speech like that one; instead, they'll be exposed to competing laundry lists of wonderful accomplishments to come. The question is, which candidate do they think is more capable of getting the job done?

When Joe Biden was sworn in as president on January 20, 2021, it was 48 years since he was first elected to the U.S. Senate. To put things in perspective, it's been so long since Biden first joined the Senate that he served with several senators there who were born in the 1800s! There's no arguing that he's been in and around Washington, DC longer than any other candidate who ran in 2020, and is one of the most politically experienced individuals ever to seek the presidency. The difference of opinion, though, is whether that's a good thing or a bad thing. Critics of Donald Trump—who prior to being elected president had never held any political office—blame some of his decisions on inexperience, and made the case for Biden as a veteran politician who knows how to govern properly. Biden's naysayers see things differently, contending that in all his time in government, Biden did very little, and so he is a proven failure.

The examples we covered in this chapter are the main reasons why people want to talk about politics. We also touched upon a reason why people with shared values and visions may argue: different priorities. In Chapter 4, we'll expand on that and explore a deeper reason people tend to argue: partisanship.

CHAPTER 4

The Burden of Party Dependence

Over the years I've amazed thousands of students by explaining to them that George Washington was *not* the first president of the United States. Actually, that's more of a technicality than anything else, but many still find it to be a fascinating bit of trivia. You see, the colonies declared their independence from Great Britain in 1776 and became the United States of America, but George Washington was not elected president until 1788. So, what happened during those first twelve years of our nation's history? Well, during the time of independence and in the Revolutionary War that followed (Britain didn't simply say "ok, you want to be independent, fine." There was a war until Britain finally relented and went home), the government in place was known as the Second Continental Congress (the first had been convened a couple of years earlier). But in 1781, with hostilities with Britain mostly concluded, the young nation established a new government under a document called the Articles of Confederation (not to be confused with the Confederacy, which was the Southern states secession that led to Civil War—that was almost 100 years later). Under the Articles, a "president of the United States" would be appointed and serve a one-year term. The first president was John Hanson (not to be confused with John Hancock, famous for signing the Declaration of Independence but who also was appointed president later on, though he could not fulfill his duties due to poor health). Others included Elias Boudinot, Thomas Mifflin, Richard Henry Lee, Nathaniel Gorham (who took over for Hancock), Arthur St. Clair, and Cyrus Griffin. But all of those presidents were more figureheads than leaders or policymakers, which is a big reason why most Americans have never heard of them. Under the Articles, the states had a disproportionate amount of power and the federal government was ineffective, and so the Founders got together in Philadelphia and created ("framed," which is why they're known as the Framers) a new form of government, based on a Constitution, which remains effective to this day. Under that Constitution, George Washington is our first president, and that's when we begin the count, all the way to, as of this writing, Joe Biden at number 46.

That trivia tidbit aside, for all intents and purposes of what we consider a president to be, George Washington was our first and unquestionably our most popular (though, even he had his critics, not least among which was our third president, Thomas Jefferson). Although the states were not particularly interested in living under one big tent—after the war they wanted to tend to themselves and have very few things in common as a country—they were united in their wanting Washington to lead that country. He was respected for his command as a general on the battlefield, and for his integrity and strong character. In fact, they asked him if he wanted to be king, and he basically told them that we had just fought a war to get away from a king (Britain's King George III), so the last thing America needs is another king.

During his Farewell Address to the nation at the end of his second term (he could have run for an unlimited number of terms, but after leading a new nation to creation and serving as its president for eight years, he figured it was time for a rest), Washington cautioned Americans not to form political parties. Washington himself is often listed as a Federalist, which was our first major political party, and wanted a strong central (federal) government so that it would not fall apart as it almost did under the Articles. Washington had federalist ideas—as opposed to the antifederalists, who believed in smaller government and more individual liberties—and so he was dubbed a Federalist by default. But Washington never joined the Federalists because he feared that partisanship would lead to power-driven groupthink and mudslinging instead of unity in steering the new nation forward. As much as his fellow Americans respected Washington, as soon as he retired they ignored his advice. The antifederalists countered with a party of their own, the Democratic-Republicans (not directly linked to today's Democrats or Republicans), and its standard-bearer, Thomas Jefferson, fought hard with the Federalist leader John Adams. Two bitter presidential campaigns, in 1796 and 1800, saw the first go to Adams and the rematch to Jefferson, and ugly divisiveness in American politics was underway. The feud had little to do with personality and character, and was almost entirely about ideology. Federalist Adams and Democratic-Republican Jefferson represented the origins of what remains today as the seemingly endless debate about big or small government.

Big vs. Small Government, Explained

Let's begin with this phrase: "we, the people, are the bosses." We are in charge of the United States. The president, Congress, the governors, mayors, state legislatures, and city councils are our hired hands. They are our maids, our butlers, and our housekeepers. We hire them, and we can fire them. Their campaigns are job interviews, and their reelection bids are performance evaluations. We can tell them what to do and how to spend our money—because it's not their money, they don't have any. We do. We give them money in the form of taxes so they can go shopping for us and buy us roads, bridges, and armies. The question is: how good of a shopper are they?

Consider this example: you spend about $200 every week on "stuff," which includes milk, bread, toothpaste, shampoo, gas for the car, etc. You determine that you want to get more stuff for your money, and so you decide to hire a personal shopper. Your choices are two of your good friends: Kristen, or Dave. Let's say you go with Kristen, who is a smart shopper. Kristen looks for good bargains, does her research before making a purchase, comparison shops, and makes sure to buy all of the essentials first, before splurging on fun things. You turn over your $200 to Kristen, and she brings home an amazing array of items. You have more groceries than you ever imagined you could buy for $200, and money left over! "Wow!" you exclaim: "Kristen, you are awesome! The smartest thing I ever did was hire you as my personal shopper!" But what if you had gone with Dave instead, who is a notorious spender? You give Dave $200 and he returns with just three items, all in one bag. "Is that all you bought?" you ask Dave. "Well," Dave explains: "I found this really great bottle of French wine on sale for $180, and you can't have good French wine without good cheese, so I got this big piece of imported French cheese for $18, and I had two dollars left and I bought a loaf of bread that was on sale. Aren't you proud of me?" You take a deep breath, gather your thoughts, and respond: "Thank you, Dave. This all looks really good, but after we eat the bread and the cheese and drink the wine, what are we going to do for food tomorrow, and the next day, and the day after that? And what about gas for the car?" Dave's easygoing smile disappears, and he looks at you, somewhat puzzled and aloof, and replies: "oh, I didn't think of that."

Americans who understand that the government is our shopper may think it is a smart shopper like Kristen, or a spendthrift like Dave. Those who consider the government to be a smart shopper would like to see it take a big role in solving our nation's problems, and even though people don't enjoy paying more taxes, they're willing to pay for what they consider to be good quality results. But those who think the government is more of a spendthrift would rather see the government stay out of the way, to have as small a role as possible, and to let the people keep more of their own money and solve their own problems.

I was born and raised in arguably the quintessential city of cities: New York. But I have also lived in rural villages with just two traffic lights in town, and I've also lived in the suburbs. Therefore, I have seen many different types of

American cultures up close. In New York City, we all lived in apartment buildings. I was a kid; my parents paid all of the bills. We paid rent for our apartment, and if something went wrong, we just called the superintendent ("super" for short). Leaky faucet? Call the super. Clogged sink? Super. Window stuck? Super. Lightbulb change? Ok, that one we did ourselves, but that was about as handy as we got. We took the garbage down to the basement, where there were several metal trash cans in which to dispose it. Our mailbox was with all the others, in the lobby of the building, all with locks on them. We didn't own a car; there was no need. It was New York City, and it would've been more trouble than it was worth. My mom was a stay-at-home mom during those years, and my dad took the subway (train) to work every day. The station was two blocks from the house and a block from his office. Ultraconvenient. My grade school was about four blocks from my house. Some supermarkets were even closer than that. We had a nice park across the street from my house that fulfilled all of my boyhood needs of playing ball, riding my bike, climbing rocks, and hanging out with my friends.

I first became a homeowner in the suburbs, and later in the country. My country home was the antithesis of my New York apartment. The street was barely lit. The neighbors all knew each other; there were about as many residents in my village as there had been on my one city block, which consisted of four apartment buildings. My rural neighbors didn't care much about streetlights, frequent garbage pickups, or even police or fire departments. They were happy with low taxes and being their own "government." My city and country neighbors were good people, and I have a lot of fun memories. But they were radically different in terms of their mindset. The city folks believed that the government should take care of just about everything. They trusted the media, and they trusted the big bureaucratic systems. Paying high taxes was a way of life, and in their minds led to high quality services. My country neighbors, however, mow their own lawns, change their own tires, and don't need public transportation. They don't see the need for the government to charge them taxes in order to do for them what they can do perfectly fine themselves.

The "big government" vs. "small government" debate we've heard about all of our lives, thus, really boils down to whether the people think the government is a good or a bad shopper. It has nothing to do with "good vs. evil" or anything else to do with "morals" and "values." It is merely about whether the American people trust the government to be their personal shopper, much like whether you trust Kristen or Dave in that capacity. In fact, and we will further discuss this in Chapter 5, the United States is less "red" or "blue" state-by state than it is a sea of rural red with densely populated urban blue sprinkles scattered here and there.

This may all sound like an oversimplification, as there are a host of other differences between "red" and "blue" voters, not least of which abortion, foreign policy, oil drilling, and gun rights. Nonetheless, the foundation is the overall trust in the government's ability to problem-solve.

Beltway Fever

Modernly, meaning over the last hundred years or so, Democrats more so than Republicans are the ones likely to consider the government to be a good shopper, even though there have been instances of frugal Democrats and spendthrift Republicans who buck that trend. Also, as we just mentioned, the difference between Democrats and Republicans is not as simple as the amount of faith in government. There are an array of other issues about which they differ. For the most part, politicians in both major parties have the same goals as the general public. They don't want poverty, disease, unemployment, dirty air and water, unsafe streets and borders, or unhappy citizens in general. Where they differ, though, is in *how* to solve the problem. Consider this example, to illustrate: you invite three of your coworkers—Amy, Jennifer, and Thomas—over for cocktails and appetizers one afternoon after work. As you are all sitting in your living room, they thank you for the invitation, exclaiming what a great idea the get-together was, and how they should do it more often. "Oh, it's my pleasure," you reply, "but I'm just really self-conscious about my living room." Amy jumps in: "why, what's wrong with it? It looks fine to me!" You respond, pointing out the smudged paint on one wall and the chipped paint on another. "Oh, that's an easy fix," Amy says. "You need a complete paint job, from top to bottom. Give this entire room a brand new paintjob and you'll love the way it looks. You'll think you've moved to a brand new house!" Upon hearing Amy's proposed solution, Jennifer jumps in with one of her own. "You don't really need a whole new paint job. It's more expensive than you'd think, it's very tiring and time-consuming, you're going to spill paint on the carpet no matter how careful you are," she says. "Touch-up paint is what you need. Just match the paint, touch up the chipped paint there, take some soap and warm water to that smudge on the other wall and it will come right out." Next, Thomas shouts "no, no, no, don't you see? The problem here is paint and you two are proposing more paint. Wallpaper, that's your solution! Just find a good pattern wallpaper and make sure to put it up correctly, and you'll never have paint problems again!"

As you ponder all three ideas, wondering which one makes the most sense, keep in mind that all three of your guests want to *help* you. They are not opposed to each other because one idea is good and the other two are evil. And, for the most part, that's how it is in government! Yes, the party of Donald Trump *and* the party of Nancy Pelosi *both* want to help you (I can see some of you shaking your heads, thinking "well, you're only *half* right!"). They just differ in which ideas they think are best.

In fact, there's a perfectly logical—if not justifiable—reason why they all simply don't level with us and say: "I'm a good person, and my opponent is a good person. We both want what's best for you, but we have different opinions as to what that is." Instead, they'll say things like: "if you vote for my opponent, s/he'll *destroy* America!" It's called Beltway Fever. Named after the Capital Beltway, a circular highway that surrounds Washington, DC, Beltway Fever can mean many things, but is often used to describe an addiction to political power. The theory suggests that elected officials—the president and members of Congress in particular—are so obsessed with gaining and retaining power that they'll do or say almost anything. And they learned a long time ago that the easier way to win is not to get the voters to like you, but rather to have them be absolutely scared or repulsed by your opponent.

Imagine that two business managers, Carol and June, work for the same company, and are finalists for a position that would have them work directly with Margaret, who is the company's CEO. Both candidates are aware of the other's application. June doesn't want to leave anything to chance. What if Margaret likes Carol's personality better? What if they realize during the interview they have something in common and really hit it off? A 50-50 chance of getting the job is not good enough, June decides. So, she makes up an entirely false story that Carol was fired a few years ago for stealing from her employer. June makes sure the information gets to Margaret. Now, Margaret is fuming. She tells her assistant: "make sure we don't hire Carol! She's a thief! A thief! Tell her we're not interested. Hire that other one, Jane, Jean, whatever her name is, June, that's it, June. As long as it's not that Carol!" To some extent, many politicians do the same thing. Rather than leave it to chance, they scare you into believing that their opponent is such a monster, that you need to vote for them by default.

Shackled by Dependency

About two-thirds of American voters are either Democrat or Republican, but that doesn't mean they won't cross party lines to vote for a candidate they think is better. Yet in today's supercharged tense and hostile climate, too many voters are forced to "take one for the team" and "hold their nose" to vote a lesser candidate who is a member of the better party—whichever one that is, depending on the beholder's perspective. Imagine that Donna, who is a Democrat, and Ralph, a Republican, both live in the same town. The year is 2018, and their local candidates for Congress are making the rounds, ringing doorbells and meeting the people face to face. Both candidates made trips to Donna's house and also to Ralph's. As it turns out, Democrat Donna favors the Republican candidate and Republican Ralph prefers the Democrat! Yet, neither voter is inclined to cross party lines because of the perceived greater good of electing as many party members to office as possible. Donna thinks President Trump is an absolute monster and is hoping the Democrats take back the house so they can impeach him, and hopefully he'll be thrown out of office. She likes the Republican candidate, but getting Trump out is more important for the good of America. Ralph, who loves America every bit as much as Donna does, thinks Trump is the best thing that's happened to America in decades and wants to do whatever he can to protect Trump from the Democrats' clutches. Besides, the thought of Nancy Pelosi becoming speaker of the House again sickens him. He really liked what the Democratic candidate for Congress had to say, but he's voting for the Republican. This is being shackled to one's party; acknowledging foregoing voting for the better choice all because there's an interparty war going on, and many voters don't want to give the other side an inch.

In Chapter 5, we'll visit a concept that, deep down, most of us realize is true, but for whatever reason, we often fail to see it: most people are good.

CHAPTER 5

Most People are Good

This is going to come as a shock to some readers, and many will disagree, but here goes: Democrats are *not* morally superior to Republicans, and Republicans are *not* morally superior to Democrats. Many bubble-dwellers on the left and right will have a hard time accepting this, and their first instinct will be to reject it, which is understandable given the one-sided spin diet they follow. Granted, there are specific moments in time when one party—usually after suffering a big electoral loss—may act very much like a sore loser, whereas the other party may appear momentarily morally and temperamentally superior—but one party, from its leaders to its followers, is not inherently or perpetually more virtuous than the other.

If you're fed bad story after bad story about the other side, you're bound to think they're completely (or at least mostly) bad. When that same "news" source, to intensify the contrast, then feeds you great, heartwarming feel-good stories about your side, surely you'll think there are no gray areas: it's Superman, Batman, and the Lone Ranger vs. all the bad guys. As we will discuss later, that news isn't necessarily "fake" but it is misleading. And it tends to steer people away from the idea that most people are good.

If you'll bear with me, consider this example of all the times I can recall having lost something valuable, such as a wallet or a cellphone. Probably about six times total (wallet once, passport once, cell phone four times). Thankfully, that's not a lot considering it's going all the way back to the time I was a kid, years and years ago (which translates to many thousands of days). The first time was my wallet, way back when I was in my late teens, old enough to have gotten my driver's license, which had my home address on it. I thought the wallet was gone forever, but then to my surprise, someone mailed it to my house. The cash was gone (probably not a lot), but all the other contents (my license, credit cards, etc.) were there. For all I know, the person who mailed it found it with the cash already gone, or maybe decided to keep the money as a tip. Either way, I was very grateful.

The second time was at a college where I worked, which had thousands of students walking through the halls every day. It was a company phone, and so the coworker who found it tracked the number to me and brought me the phone. He had found it on the floor. The third time was really a very lucky break! I was on a boat traveling from one Greek island to another, and I dropped my passport while holding a bunch of other things. Luckily, one of the boat's crewmembers found it, recognized me from the photo, and handed it back to me. An American passport in a foreign country is as valuable as brick made of solid gold!

In the fourth and fifth instances, I wasn't so lucky. Both involved my cell phone. One I lost in a bar/restaurant, and despite all my efforts to track it down, I had no luck. The other was when I was heading to the beach in Florida with my family, and stopped to fill up the car. While pumping gas, I placed my "murse" (what my wife jokingly calls my small leather bag containing my cell phone, sunglasses, etc.; "murse" is short for "man-purse") on the car's hood and after filling up, got in the car and drove away, losing the murse somewhere, with my cell phone in it. Luckily, my wallet was in my pocket. No one ever contacted me. However, in the sixth and final instance, I had good luck again. It was Christmas Day a few years ago, and we were returning home from a visit with friends. The murse again, but this time I left it in a shopping cart at a store where we stopped on the way home. Upon arriving home, I was distressed to realize my phone was gone, but no sooner than I set out to drive back to that store, an employee from there called my wife (having checked the last number dialed on my phone) to say that someone had found the bag with the phone in it and returned it to the store.

Now that you've probably concluded that I can't be entrusted with not losing valuable items (though in my defense, I've managed 99.9 percent of the time *not* to lose things), there's another moral to the story. An item of value was returned to me four out of six times. But "goodness" 66 percent of the time doesn't do enough justice to the "most people are good" theory.

A better example is a condensed version of one I often use in class, which can generate great self-awareness and reflection, and deeper perspective when it unfolds. Yet, the long version involves a give-and-take dialogue, and since you can't directly participate here, we'll go with the shorter mode. Imagine that you've lost your wallet. Terror grips you as you think about where you might have left it. It was when you took your kids to the playground. Your cell phone and car keys were small enough to be tucked safely into your pants pocket, but your wallet was too bulky, and so you kept it by your side on the bench where you were sitting. You then walked a few feet to the slide and tied one of your children's shoelaces, intending to return to the bench, but then you heard: "we're hungry" and so you packed them up and home you went. Now it's all coming back to you, as you sit inside your front hallway, wondering what to do. You pack up your kids and head back to the playground, nightmares running through your head: "I've got over $100 in cash, credit cards, and a spare car key! Whoever stole it is going to know where I live. Not only do they have my money, they can come by and steal my car one day!" You get back to the playground, hoping against hope that the wallet is still there, but it's gone! "I knew it!" you say out loud in frustration, convinced that your worst fears will be confirmed.

It's only natural that you'd feel that way, but ask yourself: if *you* found someone's wallet containing that person's contact information. Instead of keeping the wallet and its contents, wouldn't you call the person and return it? Call me a wide-eyed optimist, but I'm betting the answer is yes. Next, think about the 20 most important people in your life (your parents, spouse, siblings, close friends). If you can't narrow it down, make it 30, or 50. Wouldn't all of them try to contact the owner too? (If your answer is "no, they'd keep the money and credit cards," you might want to think about restocking your inner circle.) If you are like most people, you can include yourself, and 49 others, into the "of course we'd all try to get the wallet back to its rightful owner" category. That makes 50 out of 50 people. I'd say, then, the odds are pretty good that most people are good—and you've most probably just said it too.

Now that you've considered that most people are good, the odds are in your favor. Much to your delight, you get a call that evening from someone who found the wallet and tracked you down from your own driver's license. The person is happy to meet you in a public place to return the wallet, which is intact, without a penny or any other item missing!

How does this translate to politics? Most people are good, which includes most politicians, whether Democrat or Republican. Yes, that's correct. Bubble-dwellers need to realize that politicians for the most part are just like other people. Maybe presidents and other individuals in the upper echelon of the political hierarchy are notably different, but your everyday congress member does his/her own shopping, pumps gas, changes diapers, goes to church, watches sports, has cookouts, and doesn't commit burglary, assault, kidnapping, arson, or other terrible crimes. It is no more likely that your elected representative is part of a sinister plot to overthrow the government, advocate child pornography or human trafficking, or infect society with chemical warfare so as to promote globalism or radical population control, and they're not part of a religious cult that aims to spread mass mind control. They're also not looking to pocket the tax dollars you send them, ignore your health, safety, and overall well-being to line their pockets with bribe money and other perks. Why not? Because, please repeat after me: "most people are good."

None of this is to suggest that there aren't plenty of instances where politicians have done wrong. I don't just mean the run-of-the-mill talking out of both sides of their mouth to get elected, I mean some of them really do get caught committing extortion, accepting bribes, and abusing their power and thereby the public trust in countless ways. But the abuse and wrongdoing is not *systemic*, because most people are good.

Here's another reason why I shared my rather long example of losing things: to emphasize the point that even though I gave you several examples, if I were to share with you a day-by-day account of my life, you'd see how my losing valuable items, while it happened several times, is still very rare by comparison. Remember, the media doesn't report ordinary ongoings. In the next chapter, I'll tell you a little more about where I grew up. For now, consider that about ten years after I had moved out of that neighborhood, it had deteriorated into what many would describe as "one big crack den." The newspapers would report rampant crime there, yet I still had friends and family there, whom I would often visit. Every single instance was peaceful. That's because the press will report crimes, but won't run a story titled: "Peaceful Day in the Neighborhood Today; Nothing out of the Ordinary Happened." Similarly, the media will mention Congressman So-and-So's tax evasion or Senator Something-or-Other's ties to known criminals, but those are a tiny pebble in the sea of all politicians. Be of good cheer: by leaps and bounds, most of those—whether civilians or elected officials—who support Donald Trump or Nancy Pelosi are good people. Really, they are.

In Chapter 6, we'll start exploring the other side. If you're a Democrat, how many Republicans do you really know well (and *vice-versa* if you're a Republican)?

CHAPTER 6

Getting to Know the Other Party

If you'll endure reading about another personal experience of mine, I think it will help shed light on how our political views come to be, and how some of us walk on varied paths that shape those views, perhaps giving us wider perspective than others who remained on a singular narrow road their entire lives.

I grew up in New York City and the majority of my family and friends lived there or in neighboring Northern New Jersey, which were, and continue to be, solid Democratic Party strongholds. In 1984, even as President Reagan enjoyed a tremendous lead over his Democratic rival Walter Mondale and wound up winning an astonishing 49 out of 50 states in his reelection bid, there was a great deal of anti-Reagan sentiment around me. I saw it on the streets, where demonstrators would gather, I heard it in school, from professors and classmates, and at family get-togethers. Except it didn't get personal. If you supported Reagan, the Mondale folks deemed you a well-meaning but misguided babe in the woods, and the same went for how Reaganites perceived Mondale voters. Conspicuously absent from those days was the mindset of "if you vote for So-and-So, you are a terrible person, and surely you support or are indifferent to all the horrible things your candidate stands for" (which the beholder considers to be indisputable fact).

Such blind, senseless, and irrational rage essentially has kicked kindness to the curb. The foundations on which lifelong relationships were built and fortified over years and decades apparently were just houses of cards that could easily topple from a faint breeze caused by a low-speed ceiling fan. This behavior is more amoral than immoral, as the perpetrators are oblivious to its hurtful impact.

My own political beliefs were shaped from childhood, when I was far more interested in the American presidency than any kid my age I knew. I grew up in a family of Greek immigrants who had settled in New York City and were what today might be described as "old school" Democrats: they firmly believed in traditional family values, attended church regularly, and raised their children to respect their elders and to obey the law. They believed in fair pay for an honest day's work, and with their working class incomes were nonetheless quite charitable to the needy, though they strongly criticized the abuse of government public assistance programs by fraud or other unethical means. They often had animated and entertaining political discussions, but they never made it personal. Besides, the older generation (my parents, aunts, and uncles) were all of the same ideological mindset, whereas some of my older cousins became Reagan Republicans when Reagan ran for president in 1980. I first learned about the two major political parties—Democrats and Republicans—around the time of Watergate (1974), in the months before President Nixon's resignation. I remember being told by my elders that "Republicans are for the rich, Democrats care about the poor." That oversimplified perspective satisfied my grade school brain, as I thought to myself: "well, the rich already have a lot of money, it's the poor who need help, and so Democrats must be nicer people."

My elementary school was an extension of my family. Most of my classmates were also children of immigrant parents who were Democrats. As I later discovered, almost all of our teachers were Democrats as well. When Democrat Jimmy Carter challenged the incumbent, Gerald Ford, a Republican, in the 1976 presidential race, everyone I knew—family, neighbors, and friends (though the latter, like me, were too young to vote)—supported Carter. We spoke about Carter in class very fondly, and the only thing we did that was even slightly disparaging was that we, like much of America, laughed about his big teeth. I still remember that one of my friends, an excellent artist, drew a cartoon of Carter pulling out one of his front teeth auctioning it to the highest bidder. I asked another friend, who had recently arrived to the United States and spoke broken English, which candidate he preferred, and he shouted "Jimmy Carter!" Only one of my friends in a class of about 32 students said he was for Ford. "Carter wants to give jobs to black people and Spanish people!" he told me. I looked at him, puzzled, and asked him: "what's wrong with that?" He didn't want to discuss it any further, and I left the conversation wondering what was so terrible about giving jobs to blacks and Latinos who, incidentally comprised most of our class, and many of them were good friends of mine, and his (more on that later).

The day after Carter won the election, our teacher asked the entire class to write an essay, guessing for which candidate (Carter or Ford) six teachers in the school voted (herself included, and others such as the art teacher, gym teacher, etc.), and why. I still remember part of my answer: I reflected on all the teachers in the mix, and concluded that the ones I thought were "nice" voted Democratic and the ones who were "mean" voted Republican. After our teacher collected all of the essays, a bunch of us insisted that she give us the answer. She laughed and said: "we all voted for Carter."

I enjoyed that class and my grade school experience overall very much. Now, having spent the last 30 years as an educator myself, I remain more certain than ever that I received a first-rate learning experience. My teacher was great, and though I don't know what made her come up with that essay idea, I don't think there were any ulterior motives, and even her "we all voted for Carter" response was an example of her candor, not a subliminal method of perpetuating political groupthink. Nonetheless, when she explained that all six teachers had voted for Carter, my preconceived notions were further reinforced. "Well, of course they voted for Carter, who wouldn't?" I thought to myself, not realizing at the time that Carter barely won, by a slim 50-to-48 percent margin. I even thought the "mean" teachers, since they voted for the Democrat, must be nicer than I realized.

A few weeks later, the teacher set up a television in our classroom and we watched the inauguration live. We clapped for Carter and listened to his speech carefully. When the cameras panned to Ford, one classmate yelled out: "there's Ford, booo!" and the rest of us— except for the one Ford fan among us—also booed. I remember the look on the Ford supporter's face, though I was still too young to have empathized with how isolated he must have felt. As I grew older and more mature, I developed such empathy. Unfortunately, many people never evolve—they simply grow older without maturing.

By 1980, when Reagan was running against Carter, I was in high school. It was there that I first became exposed to what a Republican had to say. One kid would come in every day and sing Reagan's praises. He spoke about how the "bleeding-heart liberals were ruining this country," and he did it with wit and charisma—I thought I was watching a live version of Archie Bunker from the classic sitcom *All in the Family*. The teacher was a proud, self-proclaimed liberal who often verbally sparred with him, but in no way did any of us feel intimidated or pressured into thinking a particular way. The banter was fun, and funny. Jokes aside, though, I began to understand the Republican philosophy. I thought to myself: "wow, Republicans don't actually walk around thinking 'yeah, we're bad people, yeah, the Democrats are right and we are wrong,' instead, they really believe they are good, and they are doing the right thing, every bit as much as Democrats believe it about themselves!" That's when my grade school friend came to mind, the one who was afraid that Carter would "give jobs to black people and Spanish people," and realized that he wasn't against black people and Spanish people—after all, he, like me, had many black and Latino friends. Rather, he was critical of affirmative action policies he thought Carter would adopt, which might give persons of color an advantage over whites that my friend must have considered unfair, even unconstitutional. To hear my high school classmate, an actual Republican, making the case in person (I felt like a lifelong Floridian who has never seen snow) was an incredibly eye-opening revelation for me, and one that taught me a lesson I've never forgotten: always look at both sides of an issue.

To elaborate on that point, consider these two examples: the fertile octogenarian and the shoplifting mom. I remember the "fertile octogenarian" example from my law school days. One of our professors, in advising us how to write wills, taught us not to assume that highly unlikely events—such as a woman in her eighties giving birth to a baby—are impossible, and to make such provisions in wills anyway. If that woman was a client who wanted to write a will, our professor advised us to include a clause referring to any future children she might have. The "shoplifting mom" example is one that I came up with many years ago, and I often use in class: imagine that your mom lives in another state, and though you don't see her regularly, you speak with her on the phone quite often. You just heard a rumor her neighbors are spreading: that she's been spotted shoplifting in the supermarket! Knowing your mom as you do, that she is the finest example of honesty and integrity you can possibly imagine, you are confident that the rumors must be false. Not only does she have enough money to buy her groceries, but she is such a law-abiding person who wouldn't steal a penny, even if she were starving. Nonetheless, I'd encourage my students to check out the story anyway. Is it possible that your mom—being a human being, after all, and like anyone else subject to a changing mental state of mind—might be losing her grip on reality? Maybe she is no longer the person you know because something is physiologically wrong with her. Granted, in your mind you think the odds are one in a thousand, and it is far more likely that the rumors are false. Check out the story anyway.

The moment nowadays is particularly appropriate for voters to really examine both major parties, without necessarily feeling committed to either. After all, as we said, it's a matter of priorities and trust in who is better-equipped to deliver.

A Sea of Red with Blue Sprinkles

Back to our discussion from the previous chapter, there are "red states" and "blue states" depicting states that tend to vote Republican or Democrat, respectively. Beyond that, there are regions within each state, which range from big cities to remote countryside, with smaller towns and suburbs in between.

If you examine a red and blue map not by state but by district, you might be shocked by this stark imbalance: the vast majority of the physical land that comprises the United States is red, with only a few slivers of blue sprinkled in. Imagine being served an order of lobster bisque in a soup bowl shaped like the United States, and then your server sprinkles in some freshly ground pepper.

Those pepper flakes are the blue districts, and the soup itself is the red. However, those few blue patches in a sea of red contain more people overall. Manhattan is a prime example: New York City's most populous borough, and actually the most densely populated area of the country, easily containing well over 1.5 million inhabitants. Consider its residential neighborhood of Washington Heights, where I was born and raised. It is an area comprising less than two square miles, yet more than 200,000 people live there. Compare that to the state of Wyoming, which has a little less than three times the population of Washington Heights, yet is about 50,000 times bigger.

Even those who have not traveled much throughout our vast nation can appreciate the profound differences between a Wyoming cattle ranch and Times Square in the heart of New York City. To refer to the United States as a "multicultural nation" is true in more ways than one. To many people, "multicultural" means that there are Americans whose ancestors—whether ten weeks or a hundred years ago—lived in countries from all over the world, from Afghanistan to Zimbabwe alphabetically, or from Argentina to China geographically. But multicultural also means different American cultures within the United States. Such as the aforementioned Wyoming ranch vs. Times Square. Or the Alaskan wilderness vs. Waikiki Beach on Hawaii's island of Oahu. They drink bourbon in Kentucky, eat clam chowder in Boston, and a can of Coca Cola is "soda" in Florida but "pop" in Ohio. And at the time that people are eating "dinner" in San Francisco, they might be eating it in Omaha too, except out West it's the last meal of the day whereas in the

Midwest it's still daytime, and it's the meal before "supper."

Aside from being interesting and even amusing topics of conversation, cultural differences often formulate the perception of how Americans view the role of government, the media, and other entities of influence and/or authority. That, in turn, may very well point them to a particular side of the debate. The divide often, even if not always, falls along the lines of urban vs. rural.

"Blue" voters—the folks I grew up with in New York City—the ones who called the superintendent to fix every little problem, because the super was a paid-for service included with the rent, understood that the rent was higher than the cost of the mortgage and property taxes. It was a tradeoff: you get what you paid for, and my city neighbors for the most part were happy with their end of the deal. They are the ones most likely to demand that government solve a problem. "You're the government, fix it!" is their mantra, while my rural neighbors might say: "we'll be just fine. We just don't believe that the government is any better at fixing the problem than we are. In fact, we'd prefer for government stay out of the way and not mess things up and leave us be."

The Electoral College: Why it's Here to Stay

Keeping the Washington Heights-Wyoming comparison in mind, rural and urban voters also tend to line up on opposite sides when it comes to who should pick the president. No doubt, country life and city life are very different. Those day-to-day differences often influence how we view our form of government and our elected officials. This brings us to the conundrum in which the United States finds itself: it is one country that is really 50 mini-countries, and its "united" status began as a temporary arrangement whereby the 13 original colonies were likeminded in the sense that they wanted to rid themselves of Britain's oppressive monarchical government led by King George III. The 13 colonies were like 13 people stuck in a large elevator who don't particularly enjoy one another's company but realize the most important thing is to rescue themselves from their confinement. Just as they would likely work together to escape, so did the 13 colonies join forces to topple Britain from Colonial territory. Much like teenagers who just turned 18 and, upon realizing they were now legally adults, could do whatever they wanted, decided to move out of their parents' homes and rent an apartment. "Ok, so we're free, now what do we do?" might have been the cry of wonder of those teenagers, and the Founding Fathers.

As we already discussed, after they realized that a government under the Articles of Confederation wasn't working, they wrote the Constitution as the basis of a new government and gave the presidency actual power and authority, not just figurehead status. Many of the Framers remained steadfast in their opposition to a strong central chief executive leader, while others thought such a position was necessary for the country's long-term strength, functionality, and stability. There were ideological differences along those lines: Alexander Hamilton and George Washington preferred a stronger federal government, and James Madison and Thomas Jefferson a less overbearing one. The compromise reached about the presidency essentially amounted to the following: a person would be eligible to be president who was: 1) at least 35 years old; 2) a natural-born citizen of the United States (except that anyone who was a U.S. citizen at the time of the Constitution's ratification would also be eligible) and 3) an actual resident of the United States for at least 14 years (because a person can be a U.S. citizen but live in another country). Now, here's the part far too many Americans don't realize: the president *would not*—I repeat, would not—be chosen by the American people. To a great extent, this was Hamilton's doing, who famously said "the masses are asses" and thought the last group to which the vital judgment of choosing the president should be entrusted is the American people. Instead, each state legislature would appoint its own electors, which in each state would be equal to the number of that state's senators and representatives, and those electors would then elect the president. As a result of *Hamilton*, a hit musical about the Founder written a few years ago, many became enamored with Hamilton, not appreciating the hilarious irony that arguably he may have been the least likely Founder to acknowledge anything they had to say.

For the first few elections in our nation's history—ones that saw Washington, John Adams, Jefferson, and Madison, among others, make it to the White House—the American people generally didn't cast a vote for president, not even for show. Since that time, we the people do show up in November and vote, but it is mostly a symbolic gesture in which we express to the electors who we would like them to vote for; in fact, technically we vote for electors, even though state legislatures have the right to choose their own electors. It is these electors who comprise the Electoral College, and nowadays, they total 538 individuals, which is the total of the equivalent of 435 members of the U.S. House of Representatives, 100 members of the U.S. Senate, and three electors representing the District of Columbia (Washington, DC), our nation's capital, which has no members of Congress of its own. A majority, 270 electors, is needed for any candidate to win the presidency. If no candidate achieves a majority by the day on which the electors officially cast their ballots, which is always the Monday following the second Wednesday in December, then the House of Representatives casting one vote per state elects the president, as has happened twice to date in our nation's history (in 1800 and 1824).

Granted, the people's vote is not as meaningless as any of this may sound. "Faithless" electors, those who cast a vote that is different from that state's popular vote winner, are very rare. Nonetheless, past practice is merely past practice, and there is nothing in the Constitution preventing more faithless electors to emerge and vote for whomever they choose who is a natural-born citizen, at least 35 years old, and a U.S. resident for at least 14 years, even if he or she didn't run for president! They can choose, conceivably, Aaron Rodgers, Madonna, Robert De Niro, or Floyd Mayweather, Jr.—a football player, a singer, an actor, and a boxer, respectively—and to the best of my knowledge, none of them ever sought that office.

The other important component of the Electoral College, besides the fact that electors are chosen carefully so as not to leave the fate of the election to the public's potentially fickle whim, is that electoral victory is based on state victories, not an aggregate national total. That was done purposely by the Framers as a compromise for smaller states that did not want to give up their sovereignty to larger states. Nonetheless, larger states still maintain an advantage over smaller ones, just not as overwhelming an advantage as would be the case were the Electoral College not in place.

For example, California, the nation's most populous state with close to 40 million residents, also has the most electoral votes: 55. That's because, although each state has two U.S. Senators, House Members are allotted based on population, which means California has 53 of those. California's neighbor to the East, Nevada, only has about three million inhabitants and, as a result, a much lower number of electoral votes: six. Imagine, however, that the presidential election was winner-take-all based on total votes. In that case, candidates would presumably concentrate on states with large populations: besides California, those would be Texas, Florida, New York, Illinois, Pennsylvania, Ohio, and a few others, and states like Nevada, Alaska, Delaware, and North and South Dakota, among others, would be ignored. As it stands, however, presidential elections often result in tight electoral contests, and even the smaller states are very important.

Currently there are more Democrat than Republican voters, and so it is natural that they would favor a national popular vote, and that Republicans would favor retaining the Electoral College system. More importantly, it is extremely difficult to overturn a provision in the Constitution; it must be done so by the amendment process, which ultimately requires three-fourths of the state legislatures to approve, and it is unlikely that smaller states would concede their leverage. Therefore, whether you're for it or against it, it is prudent to realize that, unless a significant number of faithless electors emerges that would cause bipartisan public outrage, the Electoral College is not going away anytime soon, if ever.

Partisan political strategy aside, the Electoral College underscores two main components of the Framers' intent: 1) they didn't trust the people to make a direct decision in choosing the president; and 2) they didn't want to give too much power to the federal government. Essentially, the "United States" remained states that joined together for practical purposes, even though in a perfect world they would prefer to be their own mini-nations.

The Pendulum Swing

All other things being equal, the younger folks are, the less likely it is that they've been exposed to diversity of thought. Therefore, as rookies in the marketplace of ideas, they tend to cling to the first point of view that seems logical and good to them, and they preach it as inerrant gospel. If they encounter a diametrically opposed point of view they consider to be more convincing, they may back away from their original argument by swinging in the other direction, like a pendulum with the wind at its back. This is often the case with young adults entering college for the first time, whose norms are challenged by their professors. Many students radically shift their thinking and quickly denounce points of view they identified with their entire lives. A year or two later, while encountering counterpoints to their professors' views, they might swing back sharply the other way. As the years pass, they may become more attuned to the gray area of differences of opinion, and that's when the pendulum swings less forcefully.

Personality and Ideology

Usually, when people first start paying attention to politics, they are interested in politicians' personality, and even physical appearance and other characteristics, such as voice. Regarding presidents, we often vote for those we want to let into our living rooms—meaning, in our television sets—and watch them for at least four years. Famously, Warren Harding, who won the presidency in 1920, rose to national fame because observers said he "looks like a president." Presidents also win over audiences with warm, folksy stories and a good sense of humor.

Presidential candidates say a lot of things, but there's usually one slogan that is their main campaign theme, and it is positive and not partisan. Consider some of these over the past few presidencies: "Morning in America" (Ronald Reagan); "Kinder, Gentler Nation" (George H.W. Bush); "Building a Bridge to the 21st Century" (Bill Clinton); "Change We Can believe in" (Barack

Obama); "Make America Great Again" (Donald Trump). In the simplest terms, Americans hear these messages and decide whether they find the messenger appealing. Do they want to take a chance on Bush creating a kinder and gentler nation? On Obama leading us to change? On Trump making America great again? None of this has to do with ideology, which includes among other things opinions on abortion, criminal justice, the environment, taxes, foreign policy, and social values. As people get older, they tend to formulate a more solid ideology that is not likely to change, and they choose their candidates based on that ideology. When they are younger, though, the reverse is often the case; they become attracted to a candidate and are guided by that individual's personality.

Perception and Reality

As we'll talk about later on, what you think someone believes and what someone really believes are often two very different things. I already shared with you my revelation of encountering someone from another party after years of being surrounded by people supporting the opposite party. The same thing, no doubt, has happened to many of you reading this book. But if it hasn't, consider getting to know some people who for whatever reason have settled in a different political camp than you have. We'll talk more about that in Chapter 9, which provides tips on how to have a political conversation.

For now, let's turn to Chapter 7, which takes a look at the media and how it can affect our political thinking.

CHAPTER 7

Can You Trust the Media?

Young children's most influential figures are their adult role models, who are most often their parents. Beyond that, children are also considerably influenced by their teachers. We'll talk more about children and their exposure to politics in the next chapter. But what about adults and politics—who influences them?

I remember years ago explaining the "big government vs. small government" to a college freshman, probably around 18 or 19 years old, and she said: "It's really not important to me; my parents pay everything for me."

I was a young educator myself at the time, in my mid-twenties, and I think I learned a bigger lesson that day than she did: why young people don't care as much about politics. I think back to my own children—who are young, much younger than that freshman—as they, like the rest of us, are in the early stages of experiencing life under a new president. Their lives, if they change at all, are less likely to be affected than mine, my wife's, and those of adults in general. Kids have their daily routine, and for the most part, their lives are not noticeably altered depending on who's president.

That's why kids and teens usually don't take a big interest in politics. Granted, there are exceptions; I was one of them. When I was eight or nine years old I was reading and retyping presidential biographies from my children's encyclopedia. But that's not the average kid. Usually, it's adults who pay attention to politics. They are done with school and probably don't live with their parents anymore. Where, then, do they turn for political information? In great part, the media. Television, websites, social media outlets, and even the radio (mainly on the drive to and from work).

Although the country is roughly split evenly when it comes to being on the left or the right, most of the press is decidedly to the left of center. Many attribute that to an anti-Trump sentiment, but it started long before anyone gave serious thought to the possibility of Trump ever becoming president. For instance, in a 2014 survey, only 7 percent of journalists identified themselves as Republican (the major political party associated with right-of-center ideology).[1] Even so, in recent years, the playing field has begun to even, with the onset of conservative talk radio and right-leaning cable news channels that compete with "the big three" networks—ABC, CBS, and NBC. As for newspapers, of the four most influential and widely read dailies, the *New York Times* and *Washington Post* remain decidedly liberal, the *Wall Street Journal* conservative, and *USA Today* very much in the political center. In terms of media market share, the left still has a decided advantage, but the right is gaining.

Ironically, the media influences political opinion more now than when it was overwhelmingly one-sided. Although there remain more liberal media outlets than conservative ones, the ratio was far more lopsided in favor of the left in 1972 and 1984, even though in both of those presidential election years, Republicans Richard Nixon and Ronald Reagan, respectively, won an astonishing 49 out of 50 states. That's because back then, news outlets kept their opinion where it belongs, on the opinion pages (or TV segments), rather than infusing it into news stories. I've been a newspaper writer and columnist for many years, but I always made sure to keep my own opinion out of news articles and save it for my opinion column. As an editor, I made sure the same went for my writers too.

An eye-opening 2003 book by Bob Kohn, titled *Journalistic Fraud: How the New York Times Distorts the News and Why it Can No Longer Be Trusted*, methodically described how the once "paper of record" had deteriorated in quality by injecting opinion into news stories, where opinion most certainly does not belong.[2] Thinking back to 2003, what the *Times* and other news providers did was incredibly mild compared to today.

In 2020 I wrote a book called *Trumped-Up Charges!*, which is loaded with examples of media bias.[3] Far from being a "pro-Trump" book (I do not endorse him or even persuade readers to vote for him), it is largely a revelation of organized media misinformation and the erosion of journalism, which is precisely why in his Foreword, Congressman Gus Bilirakis writes that I have become "the watchdog of the media."[4] I'm not sure that I'm entirely worthy of such a laudable distinction, but I try my best. In fact, although like almost everyone else I prefer some presidents to others, I can make a strong case for how the media has treated any of Trump's recent predecessors quite unfairly. Potential titles such as *Obamaed-Up Charges!*, *Bushed-Up Charges!*, *Clintoned-Up Charges!*, or *Reaganed-Up Charges!* would not be hard to fill with plenty of examples of media malpractice. Trump himself referred to this type of reporting as "Fake News," but I think it's worse than fake: it is often technically true, but misleading. Actual fake news can be found on conspiracy theory websites of both the left and right, replete with all types of ridiculous and evidently false tales, such as a particular president being an alien from outer space, under the hypnotic spell of a demonic cult, or a secret agent of a foreign enemy who's been programmed to destroy us from within. In short, they are websites that concoct information completely out of thin air, and camouflage the craziness by inserting actual truths into the mix, and then weave the entire potpourri of sources—both reliable and unreliable—into a tangled web. Misleading news, though, begins with something that is technically true but presents it in a manner that guides the beholder to draw a certain conclusion, one that the reporter, and, more broadly, the reporter's employer, wants the beholder to reach.

The sad reality that far too many Americans either consciously or subconsciously ignore or, worse yet, privately acknowledge yet publicly look the other way, that it truly is a challenging scavenger hunt to find even a single media outlet worthy of one's trust. The less subtle newspapers and broadcast shows in particular unabashedly pick sides, and many among the masses follow them, seemingly interested only in the short-term gain than what is good for America in the long run. Much of journalism is now a popularity contest.

Most dangerous to the integrity of journalism are those media outlets whose bias is subtly infused into purportedly objective news stories, thereby tainting the accuracy of information one step at a time. It would be a false equivalency to deem the media's unfair treatment of all presidents as equal. Only the most irrational Trump-bashers would dispute that coverage of the Trump presidency has been overwhelmingly negative. Let's take a look at some of the reasons why that is the case: first, we cannot ignore that much of Trump's press wounds are self-inflicted. Whether justified or not, there's no denying that Trump has routinely antagonized the press with his "Fake News" bluster and far too seldom qualifying that with an explanation that he doesn't mean every single media outlet. He points to the media section at his rallies and says "look at those horrible, horrible people there," inciting his followers on hand to create a chorus of boos. Yet, consider the 43rd president, George W. Bush. Few would dispute that Bush was an absolutely perfect gentleman in the way he conducted himself in office. Yet, much of the media portrayed him as the devil, and in the 21st century's first decade, one would be hard-pressed to imagine that the media could possibly treat anyone any worse. They used the true-and-tried maneuver of comparing him unfavorably to the last Republican they picked on—Bush's father, and before that, Ronald Reagan. Then, when Alaska Gov. Sarah Palin became Sen. John McCain's (AZ) running mate in the 2008 presidential election, Bush was no longer the media's resident village idiot, with many faux-lamenting "if only she was half as smart as George W. Bush!" Again, this is not to give the right-leaning media a pass; they, too, can be inappropriately biased and have demonstrated that on many occasions.

In addition to numbers, the left-leaning media also has another advantage: subtlety. Rather than attacking the object of its aversion with a sledgehammer, they inflict a slower, more gradual death by a thousand cuts. Consider, for example, the aforementioned younger President Bush, who was an avid runner during much of his time in office. The media used to follow him during his morning exercise regimen, reporters constantly snapping high-speed photos. Depending on the exact moment one photo might have appeared flattering (chest out, smiling, strong, confident) and another, taken just two seconds later, unflattering (exhaling, slumping, sweaty, tired, overwhelmed, defeated). Just the mere act of selecting which of those two photos to publish is a calculated tactic, the goal being to depict the president in a particular manner. Too much artificially induced imaging, whether positive or negative, erodes media integrity.

An even more serious example of journalistic malpractice is the greatly misleading accusation by much of the media that Trump, in his announcement to run for president in June, 2015, "called Mexicans 'rapists' and 'criminals.'" I devoted a whole chapter to this topic in *Trumped-Up Charges!*; here's a shorter version: the exact language he used that day, June 16, live from Trump Tower, was: "When Mexico sends its people, they're not sending their best. They're not sending you. They're not sending you. They're sending people that have lots of problems, and they're bringing those problems with us. They're bringing drugs. They're bringing crime. They're rapists. And some, I assume, are good people. But I speak to border guards and they tell us what we're getting. And it only makes common sense. It only makes common sense. They're sending us not the right people."

There were far too many "Trump Announces Presidential Candidacy, Calls Mexicans 'Rapists' and 'Criminals'" headlines, and very few that got the story right. Trump actually said that *Mexico is sending* bad people. By "Mexico" he meant the Mexican government, and the "people" to whom he was referring in many cases are not even Mexican. Trump's reasoning was that the corrupt Mexican government, rather than taking responsibility for criminals and other thugs that infiltrate its own country, enable these bad guys to travel further north, into the United States. If anyone ought to be offended, it's the Mexican government of 2015, not the entire population of Mexicans. Without detracting too far from the main point, Trump's argument about the Mexican government was not particularly far-fetched, for two main reasons. First, an article published in the *New York Times*, which is certainly not a Trump fan, reporting that the Mexican government published a pamphlet instructing how to cross over to the United States illegally and live there without being detected.[5] Written in January 2005, the article states that the Mexican government printed and distributed 1.5 million copies of the pamphlet in the previous month.[6] At the time, the Mexican government conceded to publishing the pamphlet, but insisted it was not designed to encourage illegal entry from Mexico into the United States, but rather to save the lives of those who would attempt such a dangerous journey. The pamphlet also provided tips on how not to get caught once living in the United States illegally, for example, by avoiding loud parties or nightclubs that might be raided by police. Second, Transparency International, the leading global nonprofit committed to fighting government corruption in all countries throughout the world, in 2015 ranked 168 countries and territories on a scale of 0 (highly corrupt) to 100 (very clean), and Mexico scored a mere 31, tying with Honduras, Mauritania, Malawe, Mozambique, and Vietnam for 111th on the list, well below the international average.[7]

The examples of the *Times* article and Transparency International's report are not meant to argue that Trump's claim about Mexico's government being corrupt is unequivocally true, but only to demonstrate that he didn't simply concoct the idea in his head. The bigger point, however, is that even if this was some nutty conspiracy theory that Trump conjured up all by himself, a more appropriate headline would have been: "Trump Accuses Mexican Government of Sending 'Rapists' and 'Criminals' to the United States."

Some would argue: "what's the difference? Isn't it bad either way?" There are varying degrees of "bad." What would most people find more offensive: 1) accusing a foreign government—which was already internationally ranked for having high levels of corruption—of corrupt activity? Or 2) labeling an entire nationality of people rapists and criminals? Obviously, the second is worse than the first, and it is misleading story after story that leads to the aforementioned death by a thousand cuts.

"I Can See Russia from My House"

When McCain chose Palin to be his running mate, her folksy "hockey mom" style appealed to droves of Republican voters, but many Democrats lampooned her for being completely out of touch with just about anything going on outside of Alaska, whether in the other 49 states or the rest of the world. When Palin explained that because of Alaska's proximity to two foreign countries, Canada and particularly Russia, her role in negotiating international issues such as airspace bolstered her foreign policy experience. The television show *Saturday Night Live* used the occasion to create a skit with Tina Fey—whose portrayal of Palin throughout the campaign season was resoundingly praised—responding in Palin's character that she has sufficient foreign policy experience because "I can see Russia from my house." In the subsequent weeks and months, a sizable number of Americans confused fact with fiction and really believed Palin herself had spoken those words.

Make no mistake, media malpractice takes happens against Democrats too. For years, I defended Obama against ludicrous charges that he was a "secret Muslim" and worst of all, that he was born in Kenya. That one was the height of absurdity for many reasons, not least of which there were *two* separate Hawaii newspaper announcements confirming his birth on August 4, 1961 a couple of days later. Anyone who thinks that the master plan to unleash the then-infant Obama onto the world almost 50 years later would make an excellent candidate to be mayor of Conspiracyville.

I've already started defending Biden (and criticizing him too, where applicable). For instance, rightwing media falsely accused him of saying "I'm Joe Biden's husband, Joe Biden," as part of the narrative that he's going senile. However, I've heard many people say "Jill" (Biden's wife's actual name) in a way that sounds like "Joe," and Biden's one of them. Just as many on the left scoffed at Trump's purported use of the nonword "bigly," when in fact he was saying "big-league," which is yet another American cultural regionalism that many have never heard.

One of my favorite examples to illustrate the point of false assumptions and perceptions is that of a bench-clearing brawl on April 24, 1983 during a basketball playoff game between the Atlanta Hawks and the Boston Celtics. The two main culprits were Celtics guard Danny Ainge and Atlanta center Wayne Rollins. Standing 6 feet 5 inches, Ainge would be considered "tall" in everyday life, but in pro basketball, compared to the size of the other guys on the court, he was short, svelte, and even petite. Especially compared to Rollins, whose massive 7-feet-1-inch frame earned him the nickname "Tree." People remember the scuffle to this day, often recalling how "Ainge bit Tree Rollins' finger." That's easy to imagine, particularly considering Ainge's reputation for being tough and scrappy despite his size. It's not hard to visualize Ainge seeking to overcome his size disadvantage in a fight with

Rollins by resorting to biting. Except, that's not what happened. It was actually the bigger, bulkier Rollins who bit the smaller Ainge's finger! However, because it is less likely to envision an enormous guy nicknamed Tree biting a much smaller person in a fight, people continue to get the story wrong. Similarly, a lot of folks often relay stories about Trump based on perceptions rather than actual facts.

Next, there is a very practical, self-serving reason why the media has become so sensationalized: personal survival. Given the technological explosion of the past two decades, many types of careers have either become obsolete or are quickly getting there. As recently as the 1990s, travel agents were still in demand. Nowadays, you can simply go online and book your ticket just about anywhere instantly. No need for an agent. Video rental stores were prevalent coast to coast, but now you can download or stream just about any film you want to watch. As a kid, I was thrilled when my parents bought me a set of the Encylopaedia Britannica (the "ae" is British spelling). As a college student, I spent time selling Britannica myself. Nowadays, I don't know how much demand there would be for a door-to-door encyclopedia salesperson, given the invention of something called...the Internet. Although I'm happy that Britannica has survived the digital age as those encyclopedias gave me many years of good knowledge and support, I'd think they're the exception rather than the rule.

Similarly, newspapers and even TV news shows are less vital in the age of social media. For years, many longstanding and prestigious newspapers had to shut down because people were getting their news elsewhere, and the papers could no longer financially survive. Television news outlets that focused more on delivering objective facts began to dip in the ratings in favor of more animated and opinionated if not sensationalized reporting, and so the former, not wanting to experience the same fate as their print media counterparts, forewent the traditional canons of journalism for popularity. Besides disliking Trump for personal reasons, including his open contempt for them, much of the press resented him because through his own use of social media, he rendered them as irrelevant as the encyclopedia salesperson or video rental store.

At Least Weatherpersons are Honest, if Not Accurate

An age-old question about meteorologists (those who analyze and often report the weather to the public directly): how can they be so wrong so much of the time and yet keep their jobs? First, that's not necessarily true. Let's give the weather folks a break: for every blizzard they predict that never arrives, they get 25 rainstorms correct. Nonetheless, even when they're wrong, the public doesn't think they're trying to deceive us, on purpose. There was an amusing storyline on the HBO comedy *Curb Your Enthusiasm*, in which Larry David—the show's star who portrays his character often as irrationally skeptical—suspects the local weatherman of intentionally falsely forecasting rain in order to dupe his audience and enjoy access to a local golf course without having to wait to play. That aside, viewers generally trust that if meteorologists get the weather wrong, at least they have no hidden agenda. But that's not true for the rest of the media, which consistently gets low marks for trustworthiness. In a 2020 Gallup Poll, an alarmingly high 33% of respondents stated they don't trust the media at all, while another 27% said they didn't trust it very much.[8] That's 60 percent of Americans, a clear majority. Another 31 percent indicated they had a fair amount of trust in the media, and only 9 percent responded that they trusted the press a great deal.[9]

Political Comfort Food

At the dawn of the Biden administration, Americans remain hard-pressed to find news sources they consider to be reliable. Many simply turn to their outlet of choice as political comfort food. If there is any hope of evolving beyond this type of "journalism" is it that the conditions of supply and demand would eventually control it. Just as people were enticed by hyperbolic information, at some point their bellies will start to ache from too much junk food and they'll yearn for a return to journalistic normalcy. Until then, much of our inability as a nation to sit down and discuss our political differences is because much of the media feeds us absolutist information, and so far too many people think they are 100 percent correct: of course, they're not all eating from the same bag of media junk food.

---

[1] Lars Willnat and David H. Weaver, "The American Journalist in the Digital Age," Bloomington, IN: *Indiana University School of Journalism*, 14.

[2] Bob Kohn, *Journalistic Fraud: How the New York Times Distorts the News and Why it Can No Longer Be Trusted,* Nashville, TN: WND Books, 2003.

[3] Constantinos E. Scaros, *Trumped-Up Charges!*, Seattle, WA: Kindle Direct Publishing, 2020.

[4] *Ibid*. at 10.

[5] James C. McKinley, Jr., "A Mexican Manual for Illegal Migrants Upsets Some in U.S.," *New York Times*, January 6, 2005, retrieved on November 24, 2019, http://www.nytimes.com/2005/01/06/world/americas/a-mexican-manual-for-illegal-migrants-upsets-some-in-us.html.

[6] *Ibid,* et seq.

[7] "Corruption Perceptions Index 2015 (as amended)," *Transparency International*, September 13, 2017, retrieved on November 24, 2019, http://www.transparency.org/cpi2015.

[8] Megan Brenan, "Americans Remain Distrustful of Mass Media," Gallup, Sept. 30, 2020, retrieved on Feb. 2, 2021, https://news.gallup.com/poll/321116/americans-remain-distrustful-mass-media.aspx.

[9] *Ibid.*

CHAPTER 8

Talking Politics in School

Although the media tends to influence adults more so than children, education is the reverse. Parents advise their children to "listen to your teachers" and so that mindset is instilled in them even as young adults entering college. In the most extreme cases, teachers (including college professors) impose their often strongly held political and social beliefs on their students, presenting them as incontrovertible fact and/or insisting that any notion to the contrary is preposterous and even hateful.

If you recall, in Chapter 6 I shared my experience of growing up in a Democratic environment only to have my first consistent exposure to a Republican when I was in high school. The obvious hadn't dawned on me: that people don't walk around thinking they're wrong, they all think they're right—and many have absolutely no doubt in their minds about how right they are. Having already discussed in Chapter 5 the premise that most people are good, we can logically conclude that Democrats and Republicans, each believing they are right about two often-diametrical points of view, are mostly good people who want good things for their fellow human beings and for their country as a whole.

As for my teachers, even though I described the "we all voted for Carter" comment in 1976, that teacher did not impose any political views on us in general. Some of my high school and college teachers did, and that was irresponsible, but nothing compared to what happened to me in graduate school, after already having spent several years as an educator myself.

In the years between high school and graduate school I voted for Democrats, independents, third party candidates, and Republicans, such as George W. Bush in 2000. While enrolled in a graduate course, I was astonished that our professor, in making some reference to contemporary American politics, actually said: "well, you all voted for Gore, I can't imagine anyone here voted for Bush" and then proceeded to make her point. I forget what that point was, but that "I can't imagine" line about Bush is as fresh in my memory as if it happened yesterday. I cannot believe that an educator not only would proclaim her own political affiliation so overtly in class, but would be so brazen as to suggest that it would be absurd to fathom that anyone possessing the intellectual prowess to enroll in a graduate course could possibly have voted for Bush.

Unlike the carefree days of my youth, when I worried about very little and figured my parents would always have my back and solve my problems—even in the unlikely event that my teachers might give me a hard time—I resisted the urge to speak up and say to that professor: "I voted for George W. Bush, and I'm happy he's president!" She might have been shocked to realize that I and possibly others in that class were Bush supporters, and that it was inappropriate on so many levels for her to have made that comment. Yet, I held my tongue because of fear of the possibility of retaliation on her part, perhaps consciously, or at least subconsciously. After all, if she was so out of touch as to think that a graduate student couldn't possibly have voted for Bush, she may have found it so off-putting to have a Bush supporter in her class that she may have graded me unfairly. I had absolutely no reason to suspect that might be the case, but why take the chance? It is a fear that thousands upon thousands, if not millions of students face throughout the country, and it is an absolute shame that they have to go through that. Incidentally, Bush, whom my professor couldn't imagine earning the support of a graduate student, was a graduate of both Harvard and Yale Universities, and although family connections can help procure admission, they can't ensure graduation, as sons of powerful families, such as Ted Kennedy, found out the hard way.

When Trump became president, the politicization in academia was so perversely illogical that it almost seemed like a giant practical joke. Instructors and administrators provided students with coloring books, cocoa, and cuddle puppies—no, not in Kindergarten, in college! —to alleviate their distress over the election results. Exams were canceled, the underlying message being: who can possibly concentrate with such trauma? It was as if Trump's victory had joined Pearl Harbor and 9/11 as the third major catastrophe to befall the United States in the past hundred years. I can only imagine what my graduate school professor, if she was still teaching at the time, was telling her students! I sat in on various lectures conducted by colleagues during the first couple of years of Trump's presidency, and at times I was stunned by the subtle browbeating and not-so-subtle political proselytizing. One professor's soliloquy consisted of a litany of Trump-bashing anecdotes, prompting students to raise their hands and eagerly jump on the bandwagon when called upon, sharing their own example. They were trying to outdo one another to gain the professor's favor by letting him know that they were on his side against the Trump monster, and when one student asked: "well, what can we do?" the professor did not waste any time rattling off various leftist organizations that the students ought to consider joining. Never once did the opposite point of view, one held by nearly half the nation, see the light of day.

Like their counterparts in journalism, most educators also lean left of center and tend to vote Democratic more often than Republican. If that ratio is indeed as lopsided as, say, 70/30, or even worse, then that is truly a big problem, just as big as if the reverse were true, if it was overwhelmingly conservative Republican. Actually, if educators treated all points of view with equal respect and attention, and as it affected their interactions with their students and colleagues, it wouldn't matter if the ratio was 99/1 in either direction. Consider this: if someone makes the point that "a Trump supporter has a hard time being hired as a college professor," a common reply may be: "well, that's just because it's Trump, he's in a category all by himself." But that is not the case. What if a department chair looking to hire a professor was of the same mindset as that graduate school professor of mine who, all those years before Trump, said she couldn't have imagined that anyone in our class would have voted for Bush? Would a candidate for the job who drove to the interview in a car with a "Bush for President!" bumper sticker really have a chance with a vehemently anti-Bush chair doing the hiring? The odds don't seem too favorable.

In all of my years as an educator—I've taught in every presidential election since 1996— not only have I never evaluated any student based on political affiliation, but I've also never tipped my political hand. I described each coming election in a passionate and animated way, but never injecting my own opinion as to which candidate I preferred. Sure, students willing to take the initiative and search my biography are bound to learn about my political leanings, but other than that, they'd have no clue about who I've voted for from anything I said or did in class.

If students were to ask me—and they've certainly done so on several occasions—"who are you voting for?" I answered them: "I'll tell you after the semester is over." It's not as if I keep my political views purposely hidden—in fact, my endorsements in some election years have been published in newspapers—but I do not believe the classroom is an appropriate place for a person who exercises influence and authority over the class to be politically opinionated, as it has high potential to suppress dissenters and make them feel less equal than classmates whose views are more aligned with the instructor's.

The Internet's Influence

Even as more adult learners return as students to conventional and online classrooms, the large majority of learners in the United States continues to be children, teenagers, and young adults. And young people turn to the Internet—whether on their computers, smartphones, or other gadgets—as their premier information medium. Instructor bias aside, the Internet also plays an important role in terms of influencing students' beliefs.

It's no wonder that people talk past each other, rather than to each other, because they rarely have the opportunity to talk with each other—thanks to the Internet. The invention that was supposed to make our lives easier and better has turned far too many people into social failures with abysmal interaction skills, and there's no worse time to develop bad habits than in one's youth, which makes them all the less likely to overcome later in life. Given the choice of how to have a conversation, face-to-face is usually the most effective manner. That is followed by sound, most commonly telephone or videoconference. Far less effective are emailing, texting, and messaging. Too much can get lost in e-discussions. Messages sent in ALL CAPS are perceived as "yelling" when it could just mean a mediocre typist who cannot deftly shift from upper to lower case. An exclamation point could mean anger, or sheer delight. An emoji of a smiley face could be taken the wrong way too. Someone who types "I don't think I'm being taken seriously at work" and receives a smiley face response where the emoji looks as if it's laughing out loud might have been sent as a "cheer up, you'll get through this" but may be interpreted as "haha, you and your silly childish problems!"

A centuries-old quote that has appeared in various versions similar to one another, which has been attributed to numerous authors, including Mark Twain, goes something like this: "I'm sorry that I wrote you such a long letter; I didn't have time to write you a short one." The implication is that longer writings are first drafts, filled with mistakes that are not only typographical, but more importantly, ones that don't do a good enough job of conveying the writer's intended message. A shorter letter in such case is an edited letter, one that has been reviewed more than once, and amended to better reflect its purpose. The problem with social media and Internet messaging is that it is often so quick and so emotional that there is no time to edit, and so messages sent instantly may contain an argumentative tone as there isn't sufficient time for the messenger to simmer down before pressing the "send" button. Also, because much Internet dialogue is anonymous, people have a tendency to develop "Internet muscles" because they are shrouded in their safe cocoon. Finally, because the Internet is virtually limitless and so easy to access, anyone can write anything about anyone or anything, thus sparking outrage over fabricated accusations. Never has there been a more effective breeding ground for conspiracy theorists to peddle their tall tales than the web. Educators of all learning levels should consider it a professional obligation to advise their students to question everything they read until and unless they can confirm that it originated from a reliable source.

Academic Heterodoxy

Although the term orthodox has many meanings—including a description of religious denominations—in its purest form it means likeminded thinking. It's opposite, diversity of thought, is heterodox. A couple of years ago I joined an academic organization known as the Heterodox Academy. Its purpose, as indicated on its website is to enhance "the quality of research and education by promoting open inquiry, viewpoint diversity, and constructive disagreement in institutions of higher learning."[10] To be accepted as a member, a candidate has to embrace the following statement: "I support open inquiry, viewpoint diversity, and constructive disagreement in research and education."[11]

At first, I wondered why they called it "heterodox" but it became clear from its website, which further describes the Academy's initiative as follows: "in order to address society's most intractable problems, learners must weave together the best ideas from a range of perspectives. Yet, colleges—the intended training ground for the sort of creative and integrative thinking such problem-solving requires—have become increasingly characterized by orthodoxy in what types of questions can be asked and what sort of comments can be shared in the classroom and around campus. Professors and students alike describe the toll self-censoring and threat of social censure have taken on learning, discovery, and growth. For the sake of higher ed[ucation] and all the enterprises of life that await students after graduation, now is the time to dig in and fix what's broken."[12]

I don't know much about the organization other than having attended some meetings online, but from what I know, I applaud its mission. Also, I was very impressed in my interaction with fellow members because like me, they do not tip their political hand. In an online meeting in January 2021 about how to have a classroom discussion about the January 6 storming of the U.S. Capitol building, each of us took turns speaking. As each educator spoke, I thought to myself: "Where does s/he stand on this whole thing? Does s/he think that those who entered the Capitol are heroes or traitors? That they're passionate citizens or violent insurrectionists? That this all Trump's fault, partially, or not at all? What do they think about Trump supporters in Congress who questioned the election results? Was that the right thing to do, or did it lead to all of this mayhem?" Amazingly, in comment after comment, each speaker stuck to the topic of how to discuss these events in class. They all realized that their own personal views on the subject—whatever they may be—are not only irrelevant, but can be toxic to the discussion.

My hope is that organization and others like it will continue to grow and develop. Now, if only journalists can create a similar organization dedicated to improving the media.

I've asked a friend and colleague of mine, Amanda Keating, to contribute to this book by adding a section on how to talk politics with a child, focusing on the home, which is a fitting way to conclude this chapter.

Explaining Politics to Children
By Amanda Keating, PsyD

If you were to think back to your early memories of childhood, you may recall political discussions occurring around you or with you. Chances are, even if you don't have memories of childhood, you were privy to topics about our political candidates and hot-button topics well before your parents thought you were aware. In fact, research into the topic shows us that children begin to digest political discussions at the time they begin digesting other areas of interest- early in the development of phrase speech. While most of us don't think of a three-year-old as having strong political opinions, we'd be wrong. Three-year-olds hold strong opinions on just about everything, and the average five-year-old often has a clear opinion about the president.

Families often have a lot of rules regarding political discussions; "don't mention anything political in front of Uncle Joe!" Don't talk about the Clintons in front of grandma!" There are often rules regarding what to say in front of children as well and when to say it.

How much and when to discuss politics with children widely varies. A lot of parents wait for an introduction to politics to occur within the confines of a child's American history class. Other parents dress their toddlers in campaign t-shirts and have them waving flags at the local polls.

Why Talk To Kids About Politics? Education or Indoctrination?

As mentioned in Chapter 3, the reasons we end up talking about politics vary. It may be to commiserate, celebrate, or persuade. More often, a discussion about politics with young children begins when the child makes a comment or remark about a political figure or topic.

Ask any parent why he or she would talk to their children about politics, and it is often with a plan to educate. However, as mentioned, even in the hallowed halls of some of our finest institutions educating post-graduates, political bias can happen without regard for varied opinions and perspectives. When we talk with children about politics, it's worth considering whether our intent is to provide them with a process and guidance for the evaluation of topics and candidates, or whether we simply want them to follow the party line. As much as we strive for the former, it most often looks like the latter.

Half the Nation is Not Crazy

As a trained professional, I can assure you that the majority of people are reasonable, caring individuals. Stressed, overwhelmed, busy- maybe. But crazy? No. Following a presidential election, there is a tendency for half of the country to assume that the other half the country is crazy. If we work under the assumption that it is not true, then how can so many people hold differing opinions? If we assume people are good *and* *sane*, how can their political beliefs be so divided? Consider the following example:

The Case of Sue and Mary

What ultimately leads us to create a political opinion? In general, it's a sum of our experiences, exposure (*i.e.*, indoctrination), and knowledge…and those all differ. The differences we have in perspective are largely attributed to having different lives, and because we are human, we often have a difficult time putting ourselves in the shoes of someone else. Consider the fable about three blind men who approach an elephant. They all touch it, but one believes it to be a branch, another a wall, and another a pillar. None are crazy, they are just privy to varying bits of information.

We can sometimes have a lot of difficulty seeing something from someone else's point of view. Children have an even more difficult time. Famous Swiss developmental psychologist Jean Piaget was able to determine that children often have difficulty cooperating with others because they have difficulty seeing things from another's perspective. This applies not only to abstract concepts (e.g. how Jeff might feel) but also to everyday concrete scenarios of perspective. In a famous experiment, children under the age of seven struggled to correctly identify which perspective another people might see when looking at "three-mountains." They more readily picked their own view of the mountain.

Think about how that translates to our political beliefs and choices when we all have such differing perspectives. And it goes beyond just our viewpoint. We also have difficulty understanding that this applies not only to us but to others as well.

Consider the "unexpected transfer task. Children are told a short story about two characters and the unwitting moving of some object unbeknownst to one of the characters. For example, Sue and Mary head to Sue's house after school so Mary can show her a new doll. Mary takes her doll out of the backpack, and they begin to play. Sue and Mary put the doll in one of Sue's shoeboxes and pretend it's the doll's house. Sue decides a snack would also be nice and goes to the kitchen to get them a snack. While she's gone, Mary takes the doll out of shoebox and puts it in her backpack. Mary needs to use the bathroom. While Mary is in the bathroom, Sue returns with the snacks. Where will Sue look for the doll?

About half of children between age four and five will predict accurately where Sue may look, and by age 10 nearly all will predict accurately the response. So, while preschoolers have little chance of applying reasoning to the beliefs of others. By age five, children can begin to "perspective take" (understand something from an alternative point of view) and the more experience they have, the more adept they become.

The Curse of Knowledge

Aside from the perspective taking of ourselves and of others, there is the challenge of the knowledge we possess. A variation of the unexpected transfer task was given to adults in an experiment: when adults knew the location of the moved object, it inhibited their ability to correctly identify where the person would look. In other words, even adults would have a harder time putting themselves in Sue's shoes when they knew where the doll was as opposed to just knowing it was moved.

When we learn new information, we also tend to underestimate how long we've had it and how widely known it is. In a study of this phenomenon in children, researchers noted that children learned new information (e.g., the color chartreuse), the children reported that they had known it for some time, and they predicted that other children, even babies, know the same thing.

This is why it might be hard to talk about politics with Uncle Joe. Maybe he has a lot of

This is why it might be hard to talk about politics with Uncle Joe. Maybe he has a lot of political knowledge- that would really make it really difficult for him to put himself in the shoes of someone else *and* to predict how they may behave (or vote) given what they know. It's a tough cognitive exercise.

Supporting the Development of Political Beliefs and Discussions

So, how can we help to support children in the development of political beliefs? How can we help them have political discussions? By developing the following skills:

- Perspective taking: putting themselves in another's shoes

- Overcoming the curse of knowledge: putting themselves in another's shoes *with the knowledge they have*

- Sharing our knowledge: inviting them into our shoes and sharing the knowledge we have

- Sharing our thoughts: inviting them into our shoes and sharing the conclusions we've made

[10] Heterodox Academy website, retrieved on February 2, 2021, https://heterodoxacademy.org.

[11] *Ibid.*

[12] *Ibid.*

[13] Heinz Wimmer and Joseph Perner, "Beliefs about beliefs: Representation and constraining function of wrong beliefs in young children's understanding of deception. *Cognition,* (January, 1983) Volume13, No.1 pp. 103–128.

[14] Susan A.J. Birch, Paul Bloom, "Children Are Cursed: An Asymmetric Bias in Mental-State Attribution," *Psychological Science* Volume 14, No. 3 (May, 2003), pp. 283-286.

[15] Marjorie Taylor, Bridget S. Cartwright, et al., "Perspective Taking and Theory of Mind: Do Children Predict Interpretive Diversity as a Function of Differences in Observers' Knowledge?" *Child Development*, Volume 62, No. 6 (December, 1991) pp. 1334–1351.

CHAPTER 9

How to Have a Political Conversation

Welcome to the final chapter! (I hope you read the whole book and didn't jump directly to this part, but in any case, I'm glad you're here!) All of the ideas expressed in this book were designed to set the stage for developing the skill to successfully navigate a political conversation without an argument breaking out.

Think back to Chapter 3 for a moment (see, I told you that you should read the whole book before landing here): it explains *why* we talk about politics. If you already agree with your fellow conversant, then it's either going to be a gripe session about the other side, or a lovefest about your own. But if your conversation is with someone of a different point of view, then this chapter will be especially valuable.

Let's remember some of the other things we discussed in this book, which will help you better understand your interlocutor. Let's call her Janice. Keep in mind, the odds are that you and Janice are both good people and that you both sincerely believe you are correct in your points of view, which you think are good for the nation as a whole. Just because Janice doesn't agree with you doesn't mean she is any less passionate about her beliefs, doesn't think her views are any less beneficial to the country than you think yours are, and surely doesn't think she's wrong. Therefore, it is not necessarily the case that Janice is on the fence with her thinking and all she needs is a good "wake-up call" of your talking points to sway her. Begin with a smaller goal; try to convince her that just because your political preferences are different, that doesn't make you a terrible human being.

It is Better to Be Called Gullible than Horrible

I've had recurring political discussions both in person and via email over the years with friends and family members whose political ideas are different from mine. We share the same values, but we differ on which person, or party, is best capable of advancing those values and resulting in a better America overall. Although many of them lack my "I think I'm right but I could be wrong" mindset and instead think "I know I'm right and I know you're wrong," at least they don't insult me by suggesting that my values are inferior to theirs. They simply think that if I support Candidate So-and-So, I must be duped. I must have been hoodwinked by the rhetoric. In other words, they think I'm too naïve, too trusting. Gullible. Rather than cut off discussion, I'll take that as the best I can get, for now. After all, given the two choices, I'd rather be called gullible than horrible. Of course, even though I keep an open mind with my "I could be wrong" possibility, the "I think I'm right" is usually pretty strong, especially when it comes to politics. After all, what has become a spectator sport for many in this age of 24/7 media—much like people who attend Super Bowl parties for the event, and know next to nothing about football— has been my bread and butter for decades. I'm tempted to say to them: "Really? *You* are the one who's upset with *me*? Who's the political expert here? If I were an astronomer and I told you the name of a particular star, would you question me? If I were a dentist and told you that you have a cavity, would you disagree? Then why don't you respect my superior historical and political knowledge and just take my word for it?" If I do that, though, it would end the discussion without us having gotten anywhere.

Once you achieve the status of "gullible" in your interlocutor Janice's eyes, that's progress, because at least she realizes that you're not a horrible human being.

It is simultaneously baffling and heartbreaking to see relationships between family members or close friends shattered because of misplaced political passion. Attention, Trump supporters, your sister isn't a bad person all of a sudden because she thinks Trump is a monster and Pelosi was right to go after him all along. And Pelosi supporters, your uncle is still the same nice guy he was, even though he walks around with a MAGA hat and flies a giant Trump flag in his front yard. If one person thinks Trump is really an ogre and the other thinks Trump has been the victim of scapegoating, those are *good* values! One person is condemning terrible behavior, and the other is condemning scapegoating. It doesn't matter who's right and who's wrong insofar as determining whose heart is in the right place: *both* are!

Common Ground

It may sound easy to advise people to "find common ground" in their disagreements, and too many may just say "we've tried that, it doesn't work, we *don't have* any common ground." An answer like that simply could mean they don't really understand how to go about finding common ground.

I remember several years ago when Barack Obama was president, someone asked Sean Hannity on his Fox television show to say something good, anything at all good, about Obama. Hannity thought about it for a moment, and replied: "he's a good father." Over the years, I've also heard Hannity say, albeit rarely, something complimentary about Obama's policies and governance, though he has been critical of Obama the vast majority of the time. Nonetheless, even a non-policy compliment such as "he's a good father" is a start.

I have been a common ground seeker for decades, because of my tremendous respect for the office of the presidency. I have proclaimed myself "Defender of Presidents" even though I certainly defend some more strongly than others, because I think all of them from time to time have been unfairly targeted by the media, academia, Hollywood, their political opponents, and the public. During the Obama years, I've heard from several friends, family members, and other acquaintances of mine who are staunch Obama critics say—usually as a result of my prodding—something complimentary about him. One friend often praised Obama's use of the military, particularly drones, in combating terrorism, and another lauded his administration's aggressive deportation of PHIs (Persons Here Illegally) with criminal records.

I asked the same question of my Democrat friends once Trump took office, to say something good about him, and the answers ranged from the snarky "well, I don't think he drowns kittens" to the more sincere "he has made other NATO members pay their fair share (NOTE: NATO is the North Atlantic Treaty Organization, a military alliance of which the United States is a member; Trump compelled other members to increase their disproportionately low contributions).

A good place to start would be with Trump's tweets. He has gotten in trouble with so many people for the tone he takes when tweeting, and as of this writing is permanently suspended by Twitter for language that company has deemed to be a risk to the further incitement of violence ("further" being a reference to the January 6 Capitol breach). Yet, a careful examination of his prolific Twitter anthology will reveal even to the most ardent critic that most of his tweets would be considered objectively benign. For example, on December 7, 2020, the 79th anniversary of Pearl Harbor, President Trump tweeted a link to his Presidential Proclamation of the same day, the text of which follows (I had already obtained this *before* the Twitter ban, to include it in this chapter):

> On the morning of December 7, 1941, Imperial Japanese forces ambushed the Naval Station Pearl Harbor on the Hawaiian island of Oahu. Tragically, 2,403 Americans perished during the attack, including 68 civilians. On this National Pearl Harbor Remembrance Day, we solemnly honor and uphold the memory of the patriots who lost their lives that day—"a date which will live in infamy"—and we reflect on the courage of all those who served our Nation with honor in the Second World War.
>
> Seventy-nine years ago, Imperial Japan launched an unprovoked and devastating attack on our Nation. As torpedo bombers unleashed their deadly cargo on our

ships and attack aircraft rained bombs from above, brave members of the United States Navy, Marines, Army, and Army Air Forces mounted a heroic defense, manning their battle stations and returning fire through the smoke and chaos. The profound bravery in the American resistance surprised Japanese aircrews and inspired selfless sacrifice among our service members. In one instance, Machinist's Mate First Class Robert R. Scott, among 15 Sailors awarded the Medal of Honor for acts of valor on that day, refused to leave his flooding battle station within the depths of the USS CALIFORNIA, declaring to the world: "This is my station and I will stay and give them air as long as the guns are going."

Forever enshrined in our history, the attack on Pearl Harbor shocked all Americans and galvanized our Nation to fight and defeat the Axis powers of Japan, Germany, and Italy. As Americans, we promise never to forget our fallen compatriots who fought so valiantly during World War II. As a testament to their memory, more than a million people visit the site of the USS ARIZONA Memorial each year to pay their respects to the Sailors entombed within its wreckage and to all who perished that day. Despite facing tremendous adversity, the Pacific Fleet, whose homeport remains at Pearl Harbor to this day, is stronger than ever before, upholding the legacy of all those who gave their lives nearly 80 years ago.

On this National Pearl Harbor Remembrance Day, we recall the phrase "Remember Pearl Harbor," which stirred the fighting spirit within the hearts of the more than 16 million Americans who courageously served in World War II. Over 400,000 gave their lives in the global conflict that began, for our Nation, on that fateful Sunday morning. Today, we memorialize all those lost on December 7, 1941, declare once again that our Nation will never forget these valiant heroes, and resolve as firmly as ever that their memory and spirit will survive for as long as our Nation endures.

The Congress, by Public Law 103-308, as amended, has designated December 7 of each year as "National Pearl Harbor Remembrance Day."

NOW, THEREFORE, I, DONALD J. TRUMP, President

of the United States of America, do hereby proclaim December 7, 2020, as National Pearl Harbor Remembrance Day. I encourage all Americans to observe this solemn day of remembrance and to honor our military, past and present, with appropriate ceremonies and activities. I urge all Federal agencies and interested organizations, groups, and individuals to fly the flag of the United States at half-staff in honor of those American patriots who died as a result of their service at Pearl Harbor.

IN WITNESS WHEREOF, I have hereunto set my hand this fourth day of December, In the year of our Lord two thousand twenty, and of the Independence of the United States of America the two hundred and forty-fifth.

If we remove the dates that would chronologically determine which president issued that proclamation, it could easily have been one made by any of Trump's predecessors, all the way back to the person who was president at the time of Pearl Harbor, Franklin Roosevelt. There is no caustic language; nothing sarcastic, antagonistic, or petty. Its tone and content are eminently presidential. It is quintessential presidential lingo. Yet, there is no doubt that many of Trump's tweets do not contain the benign and dignified language most Americans expect from their president. Nonetheless, just as the squeaky wheel gets the grease, the controversial tweets get the attention.

As for Nancy Pelosi, vilified for what multitudes of Trump supporters deem an obsessive, even illegal "witch hunt" of Trump, is also infamous for many caustic tweets, but most of them are benign, such as this one on January 18, 2021: "Guided by Dr. Martin Luther King, Jr.'s transformative work, we will never stop fighting For The People, to strengthen our democracy and build a brighter, more just and equal future for all." Another example, on November 26, 2020: "As many celebrate virtually during this extraordinarily challenging time, we take a moment to give thanks for our brave service members around the world protecting our nation."

Tweets aside—because that forum is tailor-made for sarcastic one-liners—the broader lesson here is for Trump supporters to find something good to say about Pelosi, or the other way around. At first, it won't be easy to let go of the emotion, but it's ok, you're by yourself, no one can hear you or see you. Just go to a quiet place, do a little researching, and soon enough you'll actually find one, two, three, or more things they did over, say, the past four years, with which you agree! In fact, you'll be shocked to know that on some occasions, they even agreed with one another!

When I wrote *Trumped-Up Charges!* I said that my goal was for Trump to be held accountable for whatever he really said or did, and to be absolved of what he *didn't*. I bring up several examples of instances where Trump got a bum rap. But other accusations, such as his retweeting someone else's tweet referring to former Fox commentator Megyn Kelly, with whom he had a feud at the time, as a "bimbo," or his having perpetuated for years the conspiracy theory that Barack Obama was born in Kenya before finally repudiating it, are true.

If you tend to support Trump more so than Pelosi, or the other way around, go find someone with the opposite view and turn the game into a contest, where the Trump *supporter criticizes*

Trump for every time the Trump-*basher supports* him, and *vice versa* for Pelosi, thus enriching the fortress of common ground examples. The experience can be quite disarming and pleasantly cathartic. Perhaps we're getting a little bit ahead of ourselves. First, consider some other tips.

Do Not Be Insulting or Judgmental

Have you ever been a neutral third party witnessing a verbal disagreement when one person said something insulting about someone very close to the other person? For example: "Your mother is always wrong," or "your brother is a ____." Consider that person A says something about B's relative, C. In situations like that, I've later pulled A aside and said: "You shouldn't talk like that about B's relative." A would often respond: "But it's true!" to which I would counter: "It doesn't matter if you think it's true. It hurts B to hear something like that. Remember, the way B feels about C is a lot different than how you feel about C. How would you feel if B said that about one of your relatives?" At times, the A person, still not getting it, might say: "but in the case of my relatives, it wouldn't be true," not realizing the utter subjectivity of such a remark, and recalling the humorous but poignant phrase: "those who think they know everything are very annoying to those of us who do."

Of course, debates are usually about elected officials, such as the president, members of Congress, governors, mayors, etc. Granted, in most cases your disagreement will not be with any of those politicians' close friends or relatives. Nonetheless, people develop deeper affections for people they've never even met than one may realize. Consider how fanatical people are when it comes to their favorite sports teams, musicians, or even fictional characters! Imagine, then, how offended they may be if you say something horrible about their favorite politician. In order to experience a successful discussion, one that may generate worthwhile dialogue and hopefully establish a good amount of common ground, think that when you're talking about these public figures, pretend that the person with whom you are conversing is married to them and be very gentle in your choice of critical words.

Even worse is insulting your interlocutor directly. One of the worst excuses I've ever heard is: "I didn't call you stupid, I called what you said stupid, there's a difference." Actually, no, there isn't; at least not a meaningful one. It is a less extreme version of someone punching you in the nose and then saying: "I didn't punch you, I punched your nose." Simply put, the word "stupid" and similar insulting words like it should not come out of your mouth. They make you seem arrogant and utterly unlikable, and you're not likely to get very far in terms of a productive conversation.

Also, don't present as factual information speculation that cannot possibly be proven, least of all by you and those in your discussion. For instance, if you're talking about a particular president—Biden, Trump, Obama, Bush, Clinton...whomever—don't blurt out: "well, you know he doesn't really care about the country, he only cares about himself, right?" because all that will do is generate a great deal of resentment toward you by anyone who vehemently disagrees with your conclusion.

Finally, while you're being careful not to be insulting, also make sure not to be judgmental, whether toward the subject of your debate, or with your fellow debater, such as: "well, you know (So-and-So) destroyed the economy, right?" or "(So-and-So) is so divisive" are surefire ways for a discussion to deteriorate into a argument very quickly. Instead, start with a common ground point, such as: "I just hope our economy can get back on its feet again, for all of our sakes!"

Most of all, in your effort not to sound judgmental, avoid judging your interlocutor. Instead of saying: "I can't believe you support (So-and-So). Instead, ask: "I'm really curious, can you please tell me why you support (So-and-So)? I'm not being critical, I'd just like to know." Even the difference between "do you think" and "don't you think" or "is it" vs. "isn't it" is very important in terms of tone. For example, suppose you are against a proposed policy by the governor of your state, and you start a conversation with your neighbor, whom you know supports the governor. You begin: "don't you think the governor's plan will kill jobs and destroy businesses?" That may sound like a question, but it is really a judgmental conclusion clothed as a question, merely because it has a question mark at the end. Your neighbor probably perceives it as: "the governor is an incompetent jerk, whose plan is going to kill jobs and destroy businesses. You agree with me, right?" Surely your neighbor, who supports the governor, wouldn't support a policy that would ruin the state's economy, and so obviously, s/he disagrees with your assessment of the governor's plan. By asking a question in the way you did, you are already creating tension in the air, which may lead to an argument. There's a very good chance your neighbor might respond: "you don't know what you're talking about!" thereby insulting you in the process and adding to the tension, or may simply seethe silently, simply responding: "I don't want to talk about it." Time for a self-check: if by "I don't want to talk about it" you conclude that you've bested your neighbor in the argument, causing him or her to retreat because your question was so spectacular, then you really, really need to read this book. Because there's a very good chance your neighbor will storm home, fuming about what you said and how you said it.

Instead, consider opening the discussion this way: "do you think the governor's plan might not be a good thing for jobs and businesses?" Just by changing "don't you think" to "do you think" you are no longer drawing a conclusion or making a judgment. Even better, you might ask it this way: "how do you think the governor's plan may affect jobs and businesses? Will it make things better, worse, or no real difference?" By doing so, not only have you removed the judgmental onslaught, but you've also presented three choices, in this case practically a universe insofar as you wonder whether things will be better, become worse, or stay the same, and thereby, inevitably, you include your neighbor's opinion in the question. Now, unless your neighbor simply wants to pick a fight for the sake of being abrasive, s/he will probably articulate his/her point of view and a civil discussion may ensue. All because your opening remarks were inclusionary rather than judgmental.

Along those lines, I am going to share a relevant point now that impressed me so much that my only regret is not having gotten the name of the person in question, so I could thank him and praise him again. I took a trip to Washington, DC to attend Trump's presidential inauguration on January 20, 2017 I have such respect and admiration for the historical significance of inaugurations that I wish I could attend every time. In fact, I'm surprised it took me so long in my life to attend my very first one, but leaving work and family behind to travel to another city in the middle of winter isn't always an easy thing to do. Anyhow, after the inauguration, I walked around with a friend of mine searching for a restaurant to have a late lunch. Being a presidential historian and loving all sorts of presidential memorabilia, I bought a banner of the incoming president from a street vendor as a souvenir. Later on, as I walked to my car to begin my long drive home, a college-aged man, seeing that I was holding the banner, approached me and said something along these lines: "Excuse me, sir, do you support Donald Trump? I don't support him, but I'm not trying to argue you with you, I'm just really curious, what is it that you like about him?" I sensed his sincerity and responded—again, not certain of the exact words I used, but it went something like this: "I support all presidents, especially when they first take office. I want to give them a chance. What really excites me about Trump is that for the first time in a long time, we have a president who is not so closely tied to one party over the other. He won as a Republican, but even in his inaugural speech, he criticized the Republicans. When a president can criticize his own party, I like that."

The young man was very appreciative and thanked me for my time. Next to seeing a live inauguration, it was the best part of my trip, because I had a civilized, polite, and friendly political exchange with a perfect stranger with an opposite point of view. I could have raised other issues that might have been more controversial. Nonetheless, because there is much misinformation and rabblerousing by many ratings-obsessed information outlets, it is quite possible that the person might have an entirely different mindset regarding my point of view not because our values differ, but because the misinformation brigades have already made up people's minds without a chance to see and hear all of the compelling evidence.

Of course, I also made sure to touch upon the more innocuous topics, such as: to be safe from attack by foreign nations or groups, to keep our streets safe from domestic criminals, to have a thriving economy with plenty of good job opportunities, to revive our education system so that we have the top students in the world, from Kindergarten to college, etc. I avoided more controversial issues, which might push emotional buttons in others and elicit a sharper, less friendly response. Perhaps I might have addressed those topics if I had known the person well. However, because I only met him a few minutes earlier, I thought it was wise to keep it lighter.

Start with Eisenhower and Kennedy

A good way to establish common ground is to find something good to say about the other person's party, and I've found that Presidents Eisenhower and Kennedy are a great place to start. Dwight David Eisenhower (nicknamed "Ike") was one of America's most popular presidents. He was so popular, in fact, that both the Democrats *and* the Republicans approached him to run for president on their ticket. Ultimately, he chose to run as a Republican and won two easy elections, governing from the center with a steady hand. The two hallmarks that typically define a successful presidency are peace and prosperity, and the majority of the population felt both peaceful and prosperous in the 1950s under Ike's leadership. When Eisenhower left office he was 70 years old, at the time the oldest president in history (since then, that record was broken three times, by Presidents Reagan, Trump, and Biden), but his successor at 43 was the youngest ever to be elected, John F. Kennedy.[16] Eisenhower was a general and Supreme Commander of the Allied forces in Europe during WW II, and the nation, reeling from the end of that war and the plunge in to the Korean War and the Cold War with the Soviet Union (not a physical war, but a battle of wits and muscle-flexing with the looming threat of nuclear battles), felt safe with the experienced old general at the helm. By 1960, though, the country fell in love with Kennedy's youth and the optimistic promise it held for a brighter future, or as he called it, "a new frontier." A Democrat, Kennedy defeated Ike's vice president, Richard Nixon (who would gain the presidency eight years later). JFK also governed from the center, fighting for the poor, but staunchly anti-communist and pursuing economic growth through tax cuts.

What's important about Eisenhower and Kennedy is that they are not polarizing figures, especially nowadays, decades removed from when they governed. They are a good place to start in terms of saying something nice about the other party. Are you a Democrat? If so, tell a Republican something nice about Ike. And if you're a Republican, say something good about Kennedy to a Democrat. It's a good start to admitting that you don't think that 100 percent of the opposing party is bad.

Common Ground in the Media

For over ten years, liberal Bob Beckel and conservative Cal Thomas wrote a column for the newspaper *USA Today* titled "Common Ground." The column was a model of civility and a fine example for every American to follow. Incidentally, *USA Today* is a comparatively centrist publication and continues to be near the top of the list of most-read daily newspapers in America. For several years, I served as an editor for the English edition of *The National Herald*, a New York-based newspaper with an international audience covering primarily Greek and Greek-American news, and having the distinction of being the oldest foreign language publication in the United States. I co-wrote a similar column with a colleague, in which we debated American political issues with the same type of mutual respect and civility as did Messrs. Beckel and Thomas. But those types of dignified point/counterpoint columns are now the exception rather than the rule.

How *You* Can Help

Another way that you can boost the common ground initiative is to request those types of columns from your local newspaper, and various broadcast news stations. After all, if media outlets want to give the people what they want—rendering ratings paramount—and the people want common ground, then the result is obvious.

Earlier in the book I pointed out that Congressman Bilirakis dubbed me the "watchdog" of the American media. Well, if that's true, I need more watchdogs to join me. Challenge the writers and anchors, send letters to their editors and station managers. Write blogs. And don't stop with the media: expand your common ground insistence to academia and to Hollywood. As parents, make sure that your children's teachers are teaching in an evenhanded manner, and are teaching the importance of utilizing common ground as the ultimate tool for conflict resolution. Support forms of entertainment that do the same.

In case you're thinking: "well, that sounds good, but is any of this *really* going to make a difference? How is having a discussion with one person, or a small group of people, going to resolve all of the divisiveness going on in this country?" There is no magic formula. We need to do it two persons at a time, having a respectful, civilized conversation.

I used the "one person at a time" approach to achieve great results at one college where I worked several years ago. Because colleges often face the challenge of needing to boost student enrollment in order to remain financially sound, their admissions departments are encouraged to attract as many students as possible. Quite often, that results in conflicts with the faculty, especially when they encounter students who say things such as: "my admissions counselor never told me I had to write such long term papers!" It is not uncommon, then, for there to be ongoing disagreements between admissions and academics. The former see the faculty as too stringent, not realizing that the long-term financial health and sustainability of the institution depends on student retention and graduation, and the latter view the admissions folks as salespersons who will say or do just about anything to get the students to sign on the dotted line.

I encountered that type of problem at that particular institution, and I sought common ground with the head of admissions. Thankfully, she and I got along well and saw eye-to-eye in terms of the broader goals. We both held senior-level positions and understood that two large departments butting heads was not good for anyone. Once we reassured one another that we could work together toward a common goal, I advised that we each bring in one more person to the conversation. Each of us chose one of our more reliable assistants, with a special focus on the ability to discuss differences amicably, respectfully, and work in a friendly and cordial manner to achieve resolution. It was a success, as now there were four of us on the same page! Slowly, as our meetings brought all of us closer together, we continued bringing in more and more folks, until we had the two departments working together like a well-oiled machine.

That is the type of hard work each of us as good citizens ought to do, if we really want to move beyond this great national divide. It is really easy, and shameful, to fan the flames and worsen the problem; the hard work is to achieve lasting peace and understanding.

This problem won't go away overnight. But it also won't go away unless we all do our parts.

They say good is the enemy of better, but also, perfection is the enemy of progress. Every little bit helps.

CONCLUSION

The Top Five Takeaways from This Book

Thank you for taking the time to read this book. I hope you'll put many of these ideas to good use. We've covered a lot of ground, so, for your convenience, here's a summary of the top five takeaways:

1. **"I Think I'm Right, but I Could Be Wrong"**: Many people are so convinced that they're right that they can't appreciate that you think you're right just as much, and so they believe that all they need to do is tell you their side and you'll easily be converted. They have difficulty living by the "I think I'm right, but I could be wrong" motto, because they can't bring themselves to consider that they may be wrong.

2. **Sources of Misinformation:** Politicians often won't tell you "I'm a good person and so is my opponent. We both want good things for you, but we have different ideas on how to get there," because they are often so caught up in Beltway Fever, *i.e.*, addiction to political power, that in their obsession to win, they want to scare you into thinking their opponent is evil and your only hope is to vote against that person. Also, much of the media often embellishes information based on what it thinks its audience wants, transforming newspapers and news programs from trusted sources to political comfort food. Also, school instructors who recklessly allow their political opinions to leak into their lessons can be influential and intimidating, and deprive their students equal access to the marketplace of ideas.

3. **Most people are good.** They share the same good values that you do. Good people support politicians they think are good, and condemn politicians they think are bad, yet people can view the same politician through two very different lenses and sets of information. The misunderstandings stem from comments such as: "but can't you see that you're wrong? Isn't it *obvious* to you?" made by each side about the other. "Obvious" is in the eye of the beholder of conclusions drawn based on particular sources of information.

4. **One political party is not morally superior to the other.** If most people are good, that means most Democrats are good and most Republicans are good. One party does not clearly have more good people in it than the other. They all want good results—peace, prosperity, good health, happiness—but their difference is in *how* to achieve those things. Again, varying perspectives on this depend on varying sources of (mis)information.

5. **Good Manners:** Having a civilized, cordial, or even friendly conversation depends on good manners. Do not insult, do not belittle, do not mock, and do not offend. And whenever possible, have such discussions face-to-face. Text messaging and emails, unless carefully written, can seem very cold and stark. Remember, the moral high ground is not yours. Chances are, your interlocutor is every bit as good a person as you are, but with a different perspective based on his/her sources of information. Be kind. Don't let your words be hurtful. Don't make it personal. Don't destroy a wonderful longstanding personal

bond over competing perspectives about a bunch of strangers who most likely will never even know that you exist.

[16] Theodore Roosevelt was a few months younger than Kennedy when he first became president, but it wasn't through an election; he was vice president and ascended to the presidency because President McKinley was assassinated. Roosevelt then won an elected term four years later.

EPILOGUE

Kindness: A New Manifest Destiny

John Tyler was the tenth president of the United States. Most Americans have never heard of him and have no idea what he looked like, let alone what he accomplished in office. Historians often consider him in the bottom five presidents of all time, and some think he was a treasonous traitor. Tyler was such a strong proponent of states' rights that his actions indicated to a great extent that he thought of himself as a Virginian first and an American second. Even though he was long out of office, Tyler desperately tried to keep the nation together as the onset of the Civil War loomed. When Virginia seceded, he joined the Confederacy (this time, we *are* talking about the Southern secession, not the previously discussed Articles of Confederation), even being elected to a seat in the Confederate Congress, which he didn't get a chance to fill because he died. Another distinction Tyler had is that he was really the only president since Washington without a political party. Like Trump, Tyler marched to the beat of his own drum, but even though Trump was probably more critical of his own party (the Republicans in his case) than most other presidents, he never completely abandoned it. Tyler, though, had a rift with *both* major parties of the time: the Democrats and the Whigs. It's no wonder, then, he is thought of in such a negative manner, but presidents, like other historic figures, are usually more complex than that.

In Tyler's case, one of his main goals was to see through the annexation of Texas as a state. Due to its sheer size, Texas added geographic gravitas to the growing nation and launched the Manifest Destiny movement—a belief that God had destined the United States to expand from coast to coast, and therefore it was our duty to fulfill God's will. Not too many years thereafter, the United States did indeed complete its stretch from the Atlantic Ocean to the Pacific, and later added non-Continental Alaska and Hawaii, for good measure.

Manifest Destiny, then, is the idea of expanding from coast to coast. Back then, it was a physical dream; today, it needs to be a dream of spreading kindness from coast to coast. Kindness will flourish where the soil is fertile for it to take root. And what better way to cleanse the soil than by removing from it the toxin of political divisiveness?

As we discussed earlier, an ugly conflict has grown in America over the past 20 years, and by end of the Trump presidency caused more relationships among American neighbors, friends, and families to be shattered to an extent perhaps not experienced since the days of the Civil War—a conflict that was described as pitting "brother against brother." It was no longer a conversation about the best way to move the nation forward, it became personal. Trump supporters felt like strangers in their own country, not only branded "deplorable" and "irredeemable" by 2016 Democratic nominee Hillary Clinton, but also by those in their close personal inner circle! Trump critics couldn't believe that their loved ones were taken in by what they consider an obvious con artist who is a dangerous combination of evil, manipulative, and idiotic. Invitations to holiday get-togethers were canceled and "unfriending" became the norm. Conversations often boiled down to: "if you vote for Trump, that means we don't share the same values," or "don't you see that all the news you get is fake? You have TDS, Trump Derangement Syndrome!" "No, *you're* the one with TDS, Trump Delusional Syndrome. You think he can do no wrong!"

Gone from the intellectual discourse was any notion that either side could possibly be wrong. There was no room for doubt that the information each side had obtained was accurate and reliable, and thus no further jury deliberations were necessary. In their blind rage, both sides had kicked kindness to the curb, not realizing how thoughtless, insulting, hurtful, and even downright cruel they can be in the process, often to close family members and dear friends!

Have so many people really become so brainwashed that the only thing that matters is advancing an idea they are absolutely convinced is the only way to think? One final tip to simmering tensions broadening perspectives, and removing the blinders is to turn to the wise hindsight of history.

Learning from History

History is a great predictor of future behavior, because as historians since the days of Thucydides realized, it does tend to repeat itself. We already talked about how hated President Tyler was. He died in 1862 and hasn't risen too far in the presidential rankings. But do you know who the most *hated* president ever was, during the time he was president? Was it Trump? Well, being that he's fresh on everyone's mind, that would be the obvious guess. Like teenagers who say "this was the greatest concert *ever!*" after every live show they attend. Was it Obama? Well, he's the next-freshest on everyone's mind, so that's not a bad guess either. This mysterious president served during a time when security was far more lax than it is today, and even so, the government took great measures to protect him from angry mobs who wanted him dead. A major newspaper of the time described one of his most notable speeches as "silly flat dishwatery utterances of a man who has to be pointed out to intelligent foreigners as the President of the United States." That same man struggled to win the presidency, capturing barely over 39 percent of the popular vote. Another prominent newspaper wrote that his election made the United States the laughing stock of the entire world. Some thought that he was such a buffoon that he couldn't speak five sentences in a row that were grammatically correct. Was it someone obscure, like Tyler, of whom most Americans have never heard, such as, say, Martin Van Buren, Rutherford Birchard Hayes, Chester Alan Arthur, or Warren Gamaliel Harding? Actually, none of the above. Give up? It was none other than Abraham Lincoln. That's right, the president who along with George Washington shares the honor of being thought of as the "best ever." Oh, and that speech that was ridiculed for being so awful? That was the Gettysburg Address.[17] It's hard to imagine, but history also has a way of tempering emotions, especially irrational ones, with time and perspective. That's why presidential historians generally wait at least 20 years after a president has left office to conduct a complete assessment of his presidency. And even then, perspectives continue to change.

Perhaps 150 years from now, people will look back at our society and wonder what all the fuss was about. I am hopeful that we can do something about it now, so that this great divide will seem like a brief hiccup in our nation's glorious history, rather than the scourge that robbed it of its spirit. I really do think I'm right about that—but I could be wrong.

[17] The reason Lincoln was so despised was because many in the South resented him for wanting to abolish slavery, which they believed would send it reeling into poverty, and many in the North blamed him for steering the nation into a destructive, deadly civil war instead of just letting each state choose its own course. The "Silly flat dishwatery" comments were from a *Chicago Times* editorial, on November 20, 1863.

www.ingramcontent.com/pod-product-compliance
Lightning Source LLC
Chambersburg PA
CBHW022118280326
41933CB00007B/438